PREHISTORIC AND MEDIEVAL OCCUPATION AT MORETON-IN-MARSH AND BISHOP'S CLEEVE, GLOUCESTERSHIRE

edited by Martin Watts

PREHISTORIC, ROMANO-BRITISH AND MEDIEVAL REMAINS AT BLENHEIM FARM, MORETON-IN-MARSH, GLOUCESTERSHIRE: EXCAVATIONS IN 2003

by Jonathan Hart and Mary Alexander

PREHISTORIC AND MEDIEVAL REMAINS AT 21 CHURCH ROAD, BISHOP'S CLEEVE, GLOUCESTERSHIRE: EXCAVATIONS IN 2004

by Kate Cullen and Annette Hancocks

COTSWOLD ARCHAEOLOGY

Bristol and Gloucestershire Archaeological Report No. 5

By agreement with Cotswold Archaeology this report is distributed free
to members of the Bristol and Gloucestershire Archaeological Society
To accompany Volume 125 of the Society's *Transactions* for 2007

Cotswold Archaeology Bristol and Gloucestershire Archaeological Report No. 5

Published by Cotswold Archaeology
© Authors and Cotswold Archaeological Trust Ltd, 2007
Building 11, Kemble Enterprise Park, Cirencester, Gloucestershire GL7 6BQ

ISSN 1479-2389
ISBN 978-0-9553534-1-3

Cotswold Archaeology BAGAR series

1   **A Romano-British and Medieval Settlement Site at Stoke Road, Bishop's Cleeve, Gloucestershire**, by Dawn Enright and Martin Watts, 2002

2   **Later Prehistoric and Romano-British Burial and Settlement at Hucclecote, Gloucestershire**, by Alan Thomas, Neil Holbrook and Clifford Bateman, 2003

3   **Twenty-Five Years of Archaeology in Gloucestershire: a review of new discoveries and new thinking in Gloucestershire, South Gloucestershire and Bristol, 1979–2004**, edited by Neil Holbrook and John Juřica, 2006

4   **Two Cemeteries from Bristol's Northern Suburbs**, edited by Martin Watts, 2006

5   **Prehistoric and Medieval Occupation at Moreton-in-Marsh and Bishop's Cleeve, Gloucestershire**, edited by Martin Watts, 2007

Series Editor: Martin Watts
Produced by Past Historic, Kings Stanley, Gloucestershire, GL10 3HW
Printed in Great Britain by Henry Ling Limited, Dorchester, DT1 1HD

FOREWORD

The two sites reported on in this volume, the fifth in our *Bristol and Gloucestershire Archaeological Report* series, are published together as both provide significant evidence for settlement and occupation during the prehistoric and the medieval periods. Both also provide some evidence for other periods, particularly the Romano-British (including a field system and what are interpreted as stock-rearing enclosures at Blenheim Farm), but lack features such as the remains of buildings or storage pits that represent people actually dwelling on the site during these other periods.

Otherwise, the two sites are very different. Blenheim Farm, Moreton-in-Marsh, lies at about 130m AOD in the Evenlode valley on the eastern side of the Cotswold uplands, whereas Church Road, Bishop's Cleeve, is at around 55m AOD within the Severn Vale to the north of Cheltenham. Very little in the way of archaeological fieldwork has been undertaken previously in and around Moreton-in-Marsh, but extensive development in recent years in and around Bishop's Cleeve has resulted in a number of significant excavations, many of which are now published (including those to the south of Church Road undertaken in 1998 and 2004, reported on within the *Transactions of the Bristol and Gloucestershire Archaeological Society* no. 125, which this volume accompanies). The area of excavation at Blenheim Farm was to the north of the town and extended to about 4 hectares; at Church Road, the excavation area of less than 1000m² lay within the historic core of the village. Periods represented within the prehistoric are also different, with Palaeolithic, Middle Bronze Age and Late Bronze Age/Early Iron Age remains at Blenheim Farm, and Middle to Late Iron Age features at Bishop's Cleeve.

The different prehistoric periods, scales of excavation, locations and intensities of previous fieldwork mean that different approaches are required to interpret these sites. At Bishop's Cleeve the focus is very much on the local, whereas at Blenheim Farm it is possible to consider a much broader picture. The large area of excavation at Blenheim Farm allows for interpretation of the spatial patterning across the site, for example the use of space within the Middle Bronze Age farmstead, and of the notable absences, such as the lack of an associated field system. The smaller area of excavation at Bishop's Cleeve means that interpretation is largely restricted to the function of individual features, and how they relate to adjacent features excavated previously. At Blenheim Farm the prehistoric and medieval remains are put in context through comparison with type-sites and finds from across a wide geographical area, whereas at Bishop's Cleeve interpretation is largely based on considering relationships with similar remains excavated at other sites within the village.

Despite these differences both Blenheim Farm and Bishop's Cleeve provide results of significance, particularly for the prehistoric and medieval periods. There remain huge gaps in our understanding of Bronze Age and earlier settlement on the Cotswolds, of Iron Age settlement in the Severn Vale, and of the medieval development of our Gloucestershire villages and countryside, but the evidence from both of these sites allows us to continue to develop our understanding of these important aspects of the county's archaeology.

Martin Watts
Head of Publications, Cotswold Archaeology
January 2007

CONTENTS

ABSTRACTS

Prehistoric, Romano-British and Medieval Remains at Blenheim Farm, Moreton-in-Marsh

Excavations in 2003 at Blenheim Farm, Moreton-in-Marsh, revealed significant archaeological remains dating to the prehistoric, Romano-British and medieval periods. A scatter of early prehistoric worked flints included a Middle Palaeolithic handaxe and Mesolithic microliths, all recovered residually from later contexts. Later prehistoric activity fell into two distinct phases, ascribed to the Middle Bronze Age and the Late Bronze Age/Early Iron Age. Four Middle Bronze Age circular post-built structures lay within an enclosure partly defined to the north and west by a large segmented ditch. Two pairs of pits filled with burnt stone and adjacent to a watercourse, possibly the remains of a burnt mound, were also attributed to this period. Later Bronze Age/Early Iron Age pits or postholes, and a more distant tree-throw pit, were situated outside the earlier enclosure.

A Romano-British field system and associated enclosures extended across the western half of the excavation area. Some of the Romano-British ditches defining these features were evidently still visible in the medieval period, when they were reused to create a series of small ditched pens or paddocks, probably for the management of sheep flocks. A building and associated pits lay within the complex of paddocks. These were superseded by a series of larger ditched field boundaries. Artefacts suggest a broad date range of 11th to 14th centuries for the medieval occupation, with a focus of activity between the later 12th and 13th centuries.

Prehistoric and Medieval Remains at 21 Church Road, Bishop's Cleeve

Excavations in 2004 at 21 Church Road, Bishop's Cleeve, revealed archaeological features dating to the prehistoric, medieval and post-medieval periods. Prehistoric remains included a series of pits, gullies and ditches dating to the Middle to Late Iron Age, and related directly to similar features excavated previously immediately adjacent to the site. Though small quantities of Roman and Anglo-Saxon ceramics were recovered residually within later features, a second period of major activity consisted of pits and structural elements associated with domestic occupation during the medieval period, extending into the post-medieval and modern eras.

PREHISTORIC, ROMANO-BRITISH AND MEDIEVAL REMAINS AT BLENHEIM FARM, MORETON-IN-MARSH, GLOUCESTERSHIRE: EXCAVATIONS IN 2003

by Jonathan Hart and Mary Alexander

with contributions by
Wendy Carruthers, Timothy Darvill, E.R. McSloy and David Smith

INTRODUCTION

Between January and August 2003 Cotswold Archaeology (CA) carried out an archaeological excavation at Blenheim Farm, Moreton-in-Marsh, Gloucestershire (centred on NGR: SP 2080 3280; Fig. 1). The work was undertaken at the request of Crest Nicholson Residential (Midlands) Ltd in anticipation of the construction of a new housing estate. The work followed an archaeological evaluation of the site (CAT 1997) which identified a prehistoric pit as well as traces of Romano-British and medieval field systems. Following completion of the fieldwork a post-excavation assessment report was produced which found that the results of the work were of sufficient importance to warrant publication (CA 2005).

Topography and geology

The site comprises an area measuring *c.* 200m x 200m within former farmland on the north-eastern edge of Moreton-in-Marsh. It lies close to the border of two topographical zones: the Cotswold uplands, defined by Jurassic limestone deposits, and the Evenlode valley within which the site is located. Moreton-in-Marsh itself is located upon an island of Quaternary glacial sands and gravels in an area otherwise typified by Quaternary and Jurassic clays (GSGB 1981). Although the topography of the site is not pronounced, it is on a slight rise overlooking the town and is bordered along its southern and eastern sides by a stream which forms part of the fluvial system of the Evenlode. The site lies at approximately 130m AOD with ground level falling gently away to the south.

Archaeological background

Little archaeological work has been undertaken in the immediate vicinity of the site although important sites in the locality include Condicote Henge (Saville 1983), the probable Iron Age defended settlement at Batsford Camp *c.* 600m to the west (RCHME 1976, 12) and the Romano-British defended small town at Dorn *c.* 800m to the north (Timby 1998). The Fosse Way Roman road lies 200m to the west.

Moreton-in-Marsh is first mentioned in a charter of AD 714. The precise location of this early settlement remains unknown but may have been in the vicinity of the (later) church to the south of East Street, an area now known as Old Town (Leech 1981). Moreton was substantially redeveloped in the 13th century; between 1225 and 1246 a new settlement was founded along the Fosse Way with long narrow burgage plots fronting onto the road.

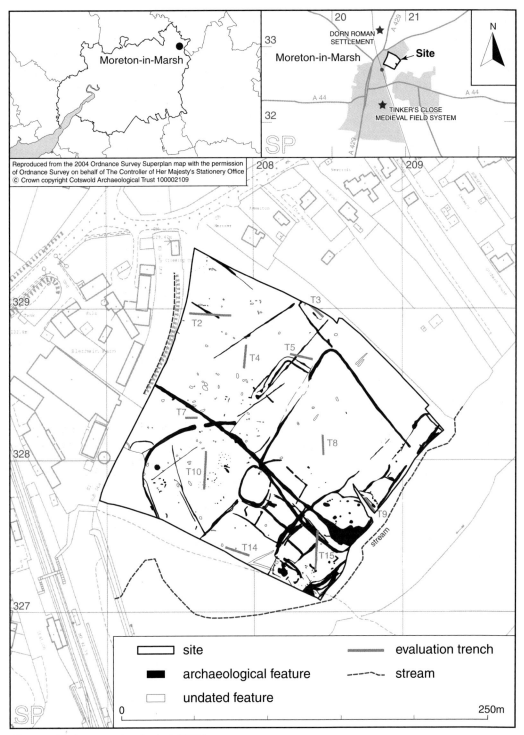

Reproduced from the 2004 Ordnance Survey Superplan map with the permission of Ordnance Survey on behalf of The Controller of Her Majesty's Stationery Office © Crown copyright Cotswold Archaeological Trust 100002109

Fig. 1: Site location plan (scale 1:2500)

Excavation in 1995 and 1996 within the town at Tinker's Close, *c.* 600m to the south of the current site, is the only major archaeological work to have been undertaken in Moreton-in-Marsh or its immediate environs before the current excavation (Langton *et al.* 2000). Prehistoric activity was attested to by the presence of residual flints recovered from medieval features, which also contained residual 1st to 2nd-century AD Roman pottery. The majority of the features identified at Tinker's Close dated from the 11th to 13th centuries and comprised three phases of field ditches and furrows. No direct evidence for the pre-13th-century settlement was identified at Tinker's Close but the proximity of occupation is suggested by the presence of several possible quarry pits and building materials, as well as finds indicating domestic activity. The cessation of agriculture on the site seems to broadly correspond with the 13th-century redevelopment of Moreton and perhaps indicates an anticipated expansion of the town into these former fields.

In 1997 a planning application was lodged for residential development at Blenheim Farm. Gloucestershire County Council Archaeological Service considered that the site had archaeological potential given its proximity to the medieval town and accordingly required an archaeological field evaluation prior to determination of the planning application. Nineteen evaluation trenches were excavated (CAT 1997). Two pits of possible prehistoric date were identified; one contained a sherd of prehistoric pottery and burnt stone, and a worked flint was retrieved from the second pit. No Roman features were identified, although some sherds of Romano-British pottery were found in residual contexts. Several undated ditches were interpreted as possibly associated with medieval ridge and furrow. In the light of these results a condition was attached to the subsequent planning consent requiring full excavation prior to the commencement of development.

Excavation methodology

A methodology for the excavation was detailed in a *Written Scheme of Investigation* approved by Gloucestershire County Council Archaeological Service. Topsoil and subsoil was removed from the excavation area using a mechanical excavator equipped with a toothless grading bucket under archaeological supervision. Archaeological features were then excavated by hand with sample rates of 50% minimum for pits and 100% for any deposits directly relating to funerary and domestic activity (e.g. cremations, postholes, walls, hearths, floor surfaces and floor make-up deposits). In general, 20% of linear features were excavated to provide stratigraphic relationships, to characterise feature morphology and to recover artefactual and ecofactual material.

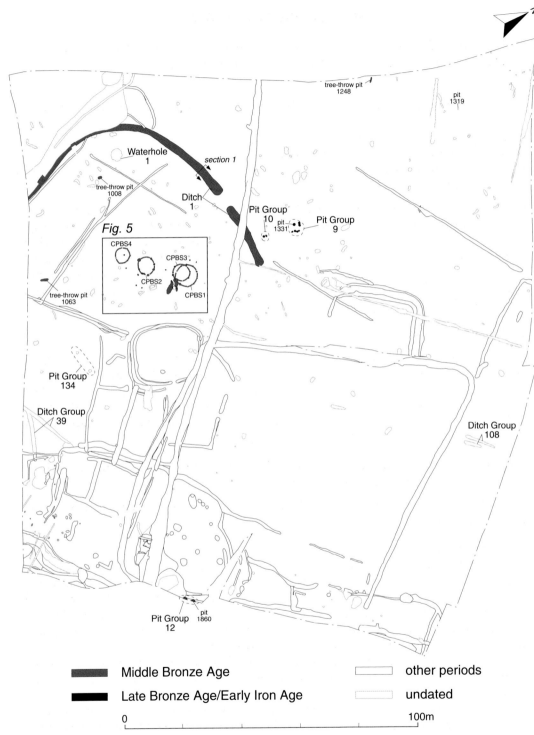

Middle Bronze Age

Late Bronze Age/Early Iron Age

other periods

undated

0   100m

Fig. 2:   Period 1, all features, and selected undated features (scale 1:1250)

EXCAVATION RESULTS

Archaeological features and deposits were found throughout the site and have been ascribed to periods within the following provisional chronology:

Period 0: Early Prehistoric
Period 1: Middle Bronze Age (*c.* 17th–14th centuries BC) and Late Bronze Age/Early Iron Age (*c.* 8th/5th centuries BC)
Period 2: Romano-British (2nd century AD)
Period 3: Medieval (*c.* 11th–14th centuries AD)
Period 4: Post-medieval (18th–19th centuries AD)
Period 5: Undated

Of these, Periods 0–3 and Period 5 are discussed below. The Period 4 post-medieval features included a field boundary depicted on the 1888 1st edition Ordnance Survey map, which ran north-west/south-east through the middle of the site and a few shallow ditches within the north-western quadrant of the site. None of these features were considered to be significant and they have not been reported on further. In the following account, capitalised features have been assigned a generic number; non-capitalised features retain their original context number.

Period 0: Early Prehistoric

Early prehistoric activity was attested to through the presence of worked flint found largely as residual material within later contexts. A Middle Palaeolithic handaxe was recovered as an unstratified find but probably came from the gravel substrate (Figs 14–15). The remaining early prehistoric material comprised unstratified and residual Mesolithic flints and included blades and bladelets, a bladelet core fragment adapted as a scraper and a burin of probable Mesolithic date (Fig. 16).

Period 1: Middle Bronze Age (*c.* 17th–14th centuries BC) and Late Bronze Age/Early Iron Age (*c.* 8th/5th centuries BC)

Period 1 activity included two distinct phases, dateable to the Middle Bronze Age and the Late Bronze Age/Early Iron Age respectively.

Middle Bronze Age (Figs 2–7)
Middle Bronze Age activity was focused on the western slope of a slight topographical rise within the central southern area of the site. This cluster of features included a substantial segmented ditch, Ditch 1; four circular post-built structures (CPBS) and two modified tree-throw pits (1008 and 1063). Waterhole 1 remained undated but may also belong to this period (see *Period 5: Undated* below). The only features firmly assigned to this phase which lay beyond this focus of activity were two stone-filled pits, Pit Group 12, on the eastern edge of the site. A number of undated postholes identified in the vicinity of the CPBSs are also likely to have belonged to this period. Pit Group 134 is undated, but likely to be contemporary in date.

Ditch 1 comprised two ditch segments forming a contour-hugging arc around the western slope of the rising ground with a 2.6m-wide entrance defined by two distinct terminals to the north-west between the two segments (Figs 2–3). The southernmost extent of

Fig. 3:   Period 1 Ditch 1 during excavation, looking west

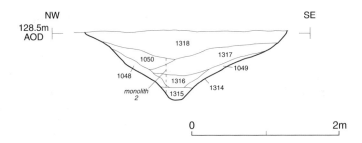

Fig. 4:   Section 1, Ditch 1 (scale 1:50)

the ditch lay beyond the limit of excavation but its alignment in relation to the extant stream just beyond the southern site boundary is striking (Fig. 1) and it is possible that the enclosure incorporated the stream into its circuit. The easternmost terminus of Ditch 1 was also distinct and no further eastward continuation was present in any surviving form. The exposed ditch segments were substantial, being up to 3m wide and 1.3m deep, but there was no indication that they had been re-cut or associated with a bank except for the slightly asymmetric middle fill of Ditch 1 (Fig. 3).

One section revealed a deliberate deposit of flint nodules, 1315, at the base of the ditch (Fig. 4). In contrast, the bulk of Ditch 1 was filled by silt deposits; pollen evidence suggests these may have accumulated rapidly in a dry environment. The deposits contained little in

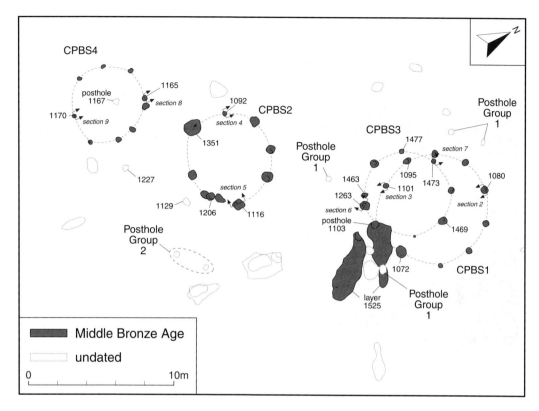

Fig. 5: Period 1, Circular Post-Built Structures (CPBSs) with associated features (scale 1:250)

the way of artefactual or ecofactual material. All three exposed terminals were excavated but none contained any notable deposits. Dating evidence recovered from the ditch was very limited and comprised small quantities of Middle Bronze Age pottery and a group of flint debitage from the primary fill as well as a few sherds of Middle Bronze Age pottery from the secondary silting. The flints were fresh, possibly indicating deposition soon after manufacture, and were probably derived from the local gravels. Moderate quantities of burnt stone, probably pot-boilers, and small quantities of burnt flint, probably the result of unintentional heating around hearths or fires, were also recovered.

Four CPBSs lay within the enclosure defined by Ditch 1 (Figs 2 and 5). CPBS1 was the largest at *c.* 7m in diameter (Fig. 6) with the remainder between 5m and 6m in diameter. All comprised a single circuit of postholes, some with post-pipes (Fig. 7, Sections 2, 5, 6 and 9). It is likely that some of the undated postholes in the vicinity were also associated with these structures. In particular posthole 1167 was located in the centre of CPBS4; Posthole Group 1 may have been the remnant of a second circuit of postholes outside CPBS1 or CPBS3, and postholes 1129 and 1227 may have been similarly related to CPBS2 and CPBS4 respectively. At least two periods of activity are represented by these structures, since CPBS1 and CPBS3 overlapped one another, although no stratigraphic relationship existed between them. Posthole 1103, which may have belonged to either of these structures, was cut through a possible buried soil horizon 1525 from which Middle Bronze Age pottery

Fig. 6: Period 1 CPBS1 during excavation, looking north

was recovered. Pottery recovered from the backfills and post-pipes of the postholes also dated to the Middle Bronze Age, and radiocarbon dates of 1450–1300 cal. BC (Wk-17813) and 1420–1260 cal. BC (Wk-17814) were retrieved from wheat grains within posthole 1101 of CPBS1. It therefore seems likely that the CPBSs were contemporary with Ditch 1. Little diagnostic animal bone was recovered from Period 1 contexts but a single sheep/goat bone was recovered from Posthole Group 2. Wear patterns suggest it came from an animal aged at least 4–6 years.

Numerous pits were located in the vicinity of the CPBSs. These were typically oval or crescent-shaped in plan with irregular edges and bases and are best interpreted as tree-throw pits. Of these, pit 1008 contained the cremated remains of an adult human while pit 1063 contained flint debitage (Fig. 2). While the remaining tree-throw pits were undated it is possible that they were the result of land clearance prior to the establishment of the Period 1 features. An undated waterhole (Waterhole 1) lay within the bounds of the enclosure. On balance it is more likely to be of this period than medieval (see *Period 5: Undated*, below).

To the south-east of Ditch 1 and the CPBSs, the ground rose slightly and then sloped down towards the stream. Two pits filled with burnt stone, Pit Group 12, were located near to the stream. Hazel charcoal and wheat grain from one of these pits yielded radiocarbon dates of 1610–1420 cal. BC (Wk-17816) and 1030–1210 cal. AD (Wk-17815) respectively; the wheat grain is considered intrusive. Two similar pits, Pit Group 134, located between the stream and the CPBSs, also contained burnt stone but remained undated.

Late Bronze Age/Early Iron Age *(Fig. 2)*
Two pit groups (Pit Groups 9 and 10) and a tree-throw pit 1248, all located to the north

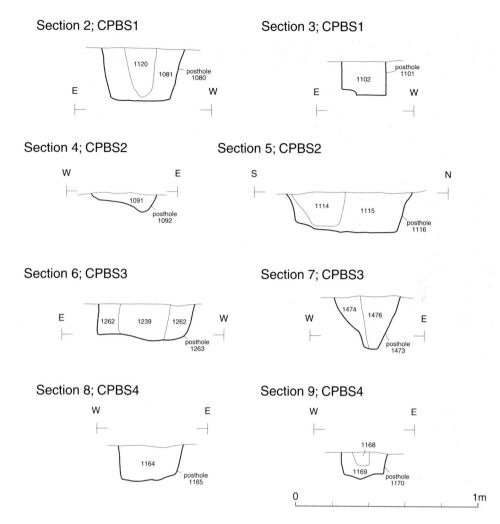

Fig. 7:   Sections 2 to 9, postholes from CPBSs (scale 1:20; all datum heights 128.5m AOD)

of Ditch 1, dated from the Late Bronze Age/Early Iron Age. The pits within Pit Groups 9 and 10 were all similar in form, being between 0.4m and 0.8m in diameter and typically 0.2m deep. Although it remains possible that these were postholes, no obvious structural plan is represented. All were filled by dark organic deposits and it seems likely that the final use of these features was as rubbish repositories. Much of the pottery recovered from these deposits was similar to the Middle Bronze Age wares recovered from Ditch 1 and from the CPBSs. However, a bipartite bowl and a bowl/jar (Fig. 17, nos 4 and 5) both from Pit Group 9 are more typical of the Late Bronze Age/Early Iron Age. Sample 29 taken from Pit Group 9 (fill 1332 of pit 1331) contained numerous hazelnut shell fragments (*Corylus avellana*), indicating that wild foods such as fruits and nuts were still an important aspect of the diet. To the north-west of these pit groups an isolated tree-throw pit, 1248, contained pottery of a similar date including a globular jar or bowl (Fig. 17, no. 6).

Field
System
1

ditch
2105

Enclosure
1

Enclosure
2

Field
System
1

Enclosure
3

Roman

undated

other periods

0   100m

Fig. 8:   Period 2, all features (scale 1:1250)

Period 2: Romano-British (2nd century AD) (Fig. 8)

Features dating to the Romano-British period were found within the western half of the site, and comprised three enclosures and a field system. The ditches were shallow (generally between 0.2m and 0.6m deep) and filled with silt deposits from which very little artefactual material was recovered. The few dateable finds comprised small abraded pottery sherds, most of which were only broadly dateable to the earlier Roman period, with a possible focus on the 2nd century AD. Although it is possible that these finds were residual within later ditches this seems improbable since, with the exception of one medieval sherd, no later pottery was recovered from any of these features despite the high level of medieval activity on the site. It is likely that the single medieval sherd was intrusive within a Period 2 deposit.

Of the three enclosures present, Enclosure 1 appears to have been the earliest. In plan, Enclosure 1 comprised an oval, measuring *c.* 26m x 20m, defined by a perimeter ditch between 0.3m and 0.6m deep, which had been re-cut at least once around its entire circuit. The eastern part of the circuit included a 0.7m-wide entrance defined by ditch terminals. Enclosure 2 was sub-rectangular in plan and slightly larger than Enclosure 1. It was defined by similar-sized ditches, some of which had been re-cut. Enclosure 2 probably formed an annexe to Enclosure 1 which was entered through a 0.9m-wide entrance along its southern circuit. The northern side of Enclosure 2 was segmented, creating two further entrances 0.6m wide and 2.4m wide respectively. The ditches of both enclosures contained little artefactual or ecofactual material and there were no dated features which appeared to have been associated with them. Field System 1 consisted of a series of narrow, shallow, field boundary ditches, typically surviving only up to 0.25m deep and laid out on a grid system based on a north-east/south-west and north-west/south-east alignment. This field system and Enclosure 3 were heavily truncated and the full extent of the ditches could not be traced. Enclosure 3 was stratigraphically later than Field System 1 but was otherwise probably broadly contemporary with the Romano-British agricultural land-use. It was defined by two parallel ditches, up to 0.25m deep, apparently forming the northern and western sides, and the south-west corner of a rectangle *c.* 34m in width and of unknown length. A possible entrance way lay on the south side. No ditches were identified along the eastern side of this enclosure although this may have been due to subsequent truncation by medieval Enclosure 5 in which soils may have been reworked to a greater depth than the area beyond the medieval enclosure to the west. Once again little artefactual or ecofactual material was recovered from the ditch fills of Enclosure 3.

Period 3: Medieval (*c.* 11th–14th centuries AD) (Figs 9–13)

Medieval activity can be divided into two phases (A and B) with a number of additional unphased features. Most of the activity at this period was focused along the western bank of the stream. Finds from these features date from the 11th to the early 14th centuries, with a focus of activity between the later 12th and 13th centuries. However, the broad date range of the pottery means that features were assigned to phases primarily on spatial and stratigraphic grounds as the broad range of the pottery did not assist with chronological differentiation.

Phase A

Phase A comprised a boundary ditch (Boundary Ditch 1) aligned north-east/south-west with a series of small paddocks or pens to the north-west. The location of Building 1 and

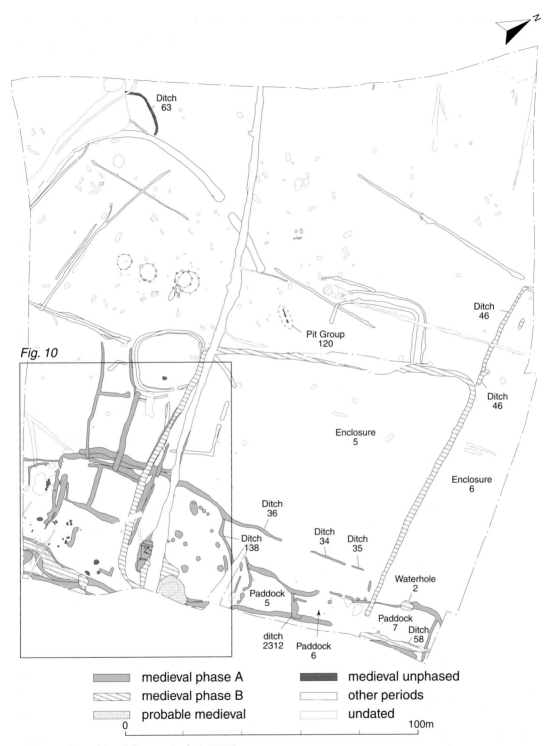

Ditch
63

Fig. 10

Ditch
46

Pit Group
120

Ditch
46

Enclosure
5

Enclosure
6

Ditch
36

Ditch
34

Ditch
35

Ditch
138

Waterhole
2

Paddock
5

Paddock
7

Ditch
58

ditch
2312

Paddock
6

medieval phase A		medieval unphased
medieval phase B		other periods
probable medieval		undated

0   100m

Fig. 9:   Period 3, all features (scale 1:1250)

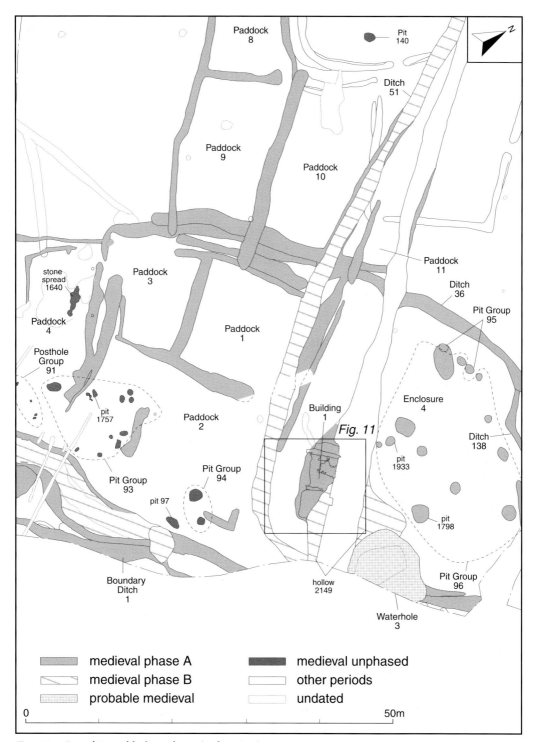

Fig. 10: Period 3, paddocks and pits (scale 1:500)

Pit Groups 95 and 96 (see Fig. 10) between these paddocks suggests that they may also have belonged to this phase.

Boundary Ditch 1 followed the alignment of the stream which ran along the eastern edge of the site. This was the lowest point of the site and the ditch, which also drained this area, had silted up rapidly and had required frequent re-cutting. To the north-west of this ditch there was a series of eleven small paddocks. The paddocks were similar to one another, each typically consisting of a small sub-rectangular plot, *c.* 20m x 10m in area, defined by shallow irregular ditches. These ditches also appeared to have silted up fairly quickly since many were re-cut several times. Moderate quantities of 11th to 14th-century pottery and small amounts of animal bone were recovered from the fills of the boundary and paddock ditches. Due to the shallow nature of the paddock ditches and the similarity of their fills, precise relationships between them were frequently difficult to establish. However, the two groups of paddocks adjoining Boundary Ditch 1 (Paddocks 1–4 and 5–7) seemed to be earlier than the ditches forming a third group of paddocks that extended at right angles to the north-west (Paddocks 8–10). While this might indicate that the focus of medieval activity shifted, in reality it is more probable that the layout of the paddocks was fluid, and subject to occasional re-establishment, modification and extension so that any perceived temporal groupings are in fact artificial.

Building 1 and Pit Groups 95 and 96 have been assigned to this phase on the basis of their location between Paddocks 1 and 2 to the south-west and Paddock 5 to the north-east. Building 1 was cut by Phase B hollow 2149. Ditches 36 and 138 defined Enclosure 4, within which these features were located, with a north-eastern continuation of Ditch 36, along with Ditches 34 and 35, possibly defining a further paddock to the north-west of Paddocks 5 and 6.

Building 1 (Figs 11–12) had been truncated along its entire northern edge by medieval hollow 2149 and by a post-medieval field boundary ditch as a result of which its plan was only partially recovered. In its surviving form Building 1 comprised two drystone walls 4.25m apart, within a wide, shallow construction cut 2238, measuring approximately 9m in length. Wall 2210 was built onto the base of the cut and comprised two roughly faced edges with a rubble core, both of limestone. It was slightly irregular in form, being between 0.55m and 0.75m wide, and survived to a height of two to three courses (0.22m). Wall 2210 was butted by the partial remains of a roughly laid limestone surface, 2237, which included an area of scorching, indicating the location of a hearth 2223. A small area of pitched stones 2224 set into surface 2237 may represent a repair. A step or platform 2221 constructed above surface 2237 and abutting wall 2210 presumably indicates the location of an entrance or internal structural feature. Silty layer 2212 covered the surfaces and butted wall 2210 and the step/platform, and contained a small amount of pottery sherds and occasional charcoal lenses. Small quantities of charred plant remains, primarily from cereals, were also present, typical of burnt domestic waste.

The construction cut dropped down slightly to the east of wall 2211, which may represent an internal division, and was built up against the face of the ledge. Subsequent truncation made the extent of this construction cut and wall unclear, however the flat-based construction cut extended up to 4.5m eastwards. The wall was 0.4m wide and survived to a height of up to three courses (0.25m) and only the eastern edge was faced. The actual form of the building remains unclear: it was overlain by spreads of limestone rubble that probably once had been standing walls, but it is also possible that the higher

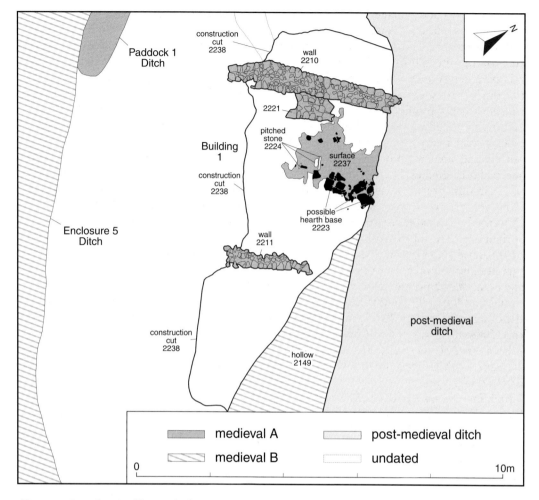

Fig. 11: Period 3, Building 1 (scale 1:100)

parts of the walls were of timber or cob construction. Pottery dating to the construction and use of the building was ceramically distinct in that it included a greater percentage of Malvernian ware as opposed to limestone-tempered fabrics, suggesting a date range of late 13th to mid 14th century. Although this assemblage appears to be later than the bulk of the medieval ceramic assemblage, the building was clearly cut by Phase B hollow 2149, so it seems likely that this difference may simply be the result of a larger group of pottery having been recovered from the building.

Pit Group 95 comprised two deep, steep-sided pits, one filled with redeposited topsoil the second with domestic waste. Pit Group 96 comprised 12 shallow scoops between 1m and 5m in diameter filled with domestic waste. Material recovered from samples <67> and <70> taken from the fills of these pits included traces of the four major cereals as well as vetches, indicating that arable resources were being utilised for both human and animal consumption. Typical for the period, they were all grain-rich with little chaff and

Fig. 12:   Period 3 interior features of Building 1 during excavation, looking west (scale 1m)

probably comprised processed grain from a mixture of crops that had been grown under quite poor conditions. The assemblages could represent grain burnt accidentally or spoilt grain that was deliberately being destroyed, indicating that the final use of these pits was for rubbish disposal.

Phase B
Features belonging to Phase B contained artefacts of a similar date range to those recovered from Phase A, but were demonstrably later on stratigraphic grounds. In Phase B the landscape was reorganised with the creation of large fields, Enclosures 5 and 6, each with a waterhole or pond close to the stream (Fig. 9). Boundary Ditch 1 from Phase A continued in use and was re-cut on numerous occasions.

Enclosure 5 was roughly square in plan, measuring *c.* 80m x 80m, and defined by a ditch which was generally 0.25m deep. The adjacent Enclosure 6 extended beyond the limit of excavation to the north-east. There was an entrance into the two enclosures by the side of the stream. Enclosure 6 appeared to be contemporary with Waterhole 2 in its south-eastern corner (the latter being stratigraphically later than a Phase A ditch). The waterhole was probably open for some time as it was filled by alternating bands of material slumped from its edges and silt deposits accumulated in standing water (Fig. 13). A turf line above one of the slumped deposits probably indicated temporary colonisation by vegetation during a dry spell and was subsequently sealed by further silting. Few finds were recovered from these deposits: no animal bone, a few sherds of 12th to 14th-century pottery, and an early 13th-century leather shoe. Insect remains from the fills indicate that it was surrounded

16

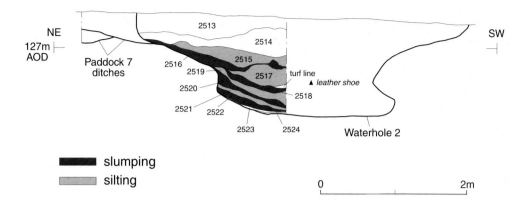

Fig. 13: Section 10, Waterhole 2 (scale 1:50)

by an open, farmed and grazed landscape. No species associated with settlement were present, which accords well with the lack of domestic waste in the waterhole. The final fills of the waterhole comprised two thick layers of redeposited topsoil, suggesting deliberate backfilling after it had gone out of use. A similar waterhole or pond, Waterhole 3, which was not excavated, was located in the south-eastern corner of Enclosure 5. The upper fill of this feature contained a late post-medieval bottle, but it is possible that the feature itself was contemporary with the medieval enclosures. Waterhole 3 appeared to be later than hollow 2149, which contained medieval pottery and which may have formed as a result of by the passage of animals down to the stream. If this is the case, Waterhole 3 may have been dug to provide an alternative source of drinking water for livestock.

Unphased

A number of features containing medieval finds could not be ascribed to any particular phase. These included Pit and Posthole Groups 91, 93 and 94 and a spread of limestone rubble, 1640, within Paddock 4 (Fig. 10); Pit Group 120 and pit 140 towards the centre of the site (Figs 9 and 10), and Ditch 63 close to the western site boundary (Fig. 9). Of these features, it is possible that the pits and postholes in the south-eastern corner of the site belong to Phase A, conceivably occupying open ground to the east of Paddock 1 prior to the creation of Paddock 2. No obvious function can be ascribed to these features, but their location close to the stream may be significant. Pit 97, next to Pit Group 94, contained late medieval pottery and may be an isolated Phase B feature, although it could reflect late backfilling of a Phase A feature (Fig. 10).

Period 5: Undated (Fig. 2)

Undated features comprised all those which could not be ascribed to a particular period on the basis of stratigraphic or spatial location or through artefactual evidence. In profile, Waterhole 1 was similar to that of medieval Waterhole 2, however, Waterhole 1 had been infilled by dumped deposits of topsoil and natural whereas the medieval waterhole had silted up naturally, with only the final fills being apparently deliberate. The material within Waterhole 1 contained no domestic waste and no finds; sample <45>, taken from one of its fills, contained no artefactual or ecofactual material other than a few fragments of burnt stone. Although this waterhole remained undated it seems probable that it was associated with the Middle Bronze Age enclosure; it was located within the enclosure and the lack of finds recovered is in contrast to the medieval features, all of which contained pottery.

Numerous undated pits were located across the western half of the site with few occurring within the eastern half. Typically these were oval or crescent-shaped in plan, up to 2m long by 1m wide with irregular or undercut edges and are best interpreted as tree-throw pits. All were filled with redeposited topsoil although those discussed under Period 1 had clearly been modified or re-used. It is unclear as to whether these tree-throw pits represent a single episode of land clearance or an ongoing process and, with the exception of those discussed under Period 1, they cannot be ascribed to any particular phase.

Ditch Groups 39 and 108 were distinctively different in form to the Romano-British or medieval ditches and Ditch Group 39 followed a unique alignment. Both Ditch Groups were filled by artefactually barren layers of silt. Nevertheless, the similarity in form between the two groups suggests that they may have been contemporary and Ditch Group 39 was stratigraphically earlier than the medieval paddocks. Pit 1319 contained a charcoal rich fill, 1320, which was sampled and contained cereal chaff. It was undated and lies at some remove from any other features.

THE RADIOCARBON DATES
by Sylvia Warman

Radiocarbon determinations were obtained from samples taken from three features (two postholes and a pit), all provisionally dated to the early part of Period 1. The main objective of the dating programme was to confirm these features as being of Middle Bronze Age date. A secondary objective was to investigate the recovery of bread wheat from Period 1 pit 1860, as this cereal is not usually found in Britain until the Iron Age or Romano-British periods, and not in abundance until Anglo-Saxon and medieval assemblages (Carruthers 2005).

Table 1: Calibrated radiocarbon results

Laboratory No.	Type	Sample <>	Context No.	Feature	Material	Radiocarbon Age (BP)	Calibrated date range (at 2σ 95.4% confidence)
Wk-17811	AMS	58	Fill 1474 of posthole 1473	CPBS3	Oat grain	913 +/- 33	1030–1210 cal. AD
Wk-17812	AMS	58	Fill 1474 of posthole 1473	CPBS3	Hazel charcoal	3080 +/- 31	1430–1260 cal. BC
Wk-17813	AMS	10	Fill 1102 of posthole 1101	CPBS1	Emmer/ spelt grain	3109 +/- 31	1450–1300 cal. BC
Wk-17814	AMS	10	Fill 1102 of posthole 1101	CPBS1	Emmer/ spelt grain	3063 +/- 31	1420–1260 cal. BC
Wk-17815	AMS	65	Fill 1861 of pit 1860	Pit Group 12	Bread wheat	908 +/- 30	1030–1210 cal. AD
Wk-17816	AMS	65	Fill 1861 of pit 1860	Pit Group 12	Hazel charcoal	3225 +/- 32	1610–1420 cal. BC

The samples were processed during 2005 at the University of Waikato Radiocarbon Dating Laboratory, Hamilton, New Zealand. All of the samples submitted were successfully dated. The results are conventional radiocarbon ages (Stuiver and Polach 1977) and are given in Table 1. All calibrations have been calculated using the calibration curve of Reimer *et al.* (2004) and the computer program OxCal 3.10 (Bronk Ramsey 2005). Date ranges are derived from the probability method (Stuiver and Reimer 1993), and those cited in the text are at 95.4% confidence level unless otherwise specified.

The results generally confirmed that the CPBS postholes and pit 1860 were correctly assigned to the Middle Bronze Age period. However, the bread wheat from pit 1860 and an oat grain from CPBS3 posthole 1473 yielded much later (medieval) dates than had been inferred by the ceramic evidence and the nature of the features. As both features also contained charred plant remains that were radiocarbon dated to the Middle Bronze Age, it is assumed that the oat and bread-wheat grains are intrusive. This is supported by the finding of a sherd of abraded Romano-British pottery in addition to the Middle Bronze Age pottery in fill 1073, another posthole fill within CPBS1.

THE FINDS

Worked flint, by E.R. McSloy

A total of 74 pieces of worked flint was recovered. Only 13 pieces derived from Middle and Late Bronze Age contexts with the majority either residual within later contexts or unstratified (Table 2). Among the redeposited flint, material of Palaeolithic, Mesolithic and Late Neolithic to Bronze Age date has been identified.

Raw material consists largely of dark or brownish-grey coloured flint of good quality. Cortex, where this survives, suggests that most material comes from 'secondary' (gravel) sources. A single light grey-coloured removal which closely resembles raw material from

Table 2: Quantification by count of worked flint by period

* = undated

Type	Period				
	1	*2*	*3*	*4*	*5**
Blade	1	2	3	1	2
Core	-	1	1	-	1
Core fragment	-	-	-	-	1
Flake/chip	5	11	15	4	5
Handaxe	-	-	-	-	1
Piercer	1	-	-	-	-
Retouched flake	-	-	1	-	-
Burin	-	1	-	-	-
Scraper	-	1	1	1	-
Total	*7*	*16*	*21*	*6*	*10*

1

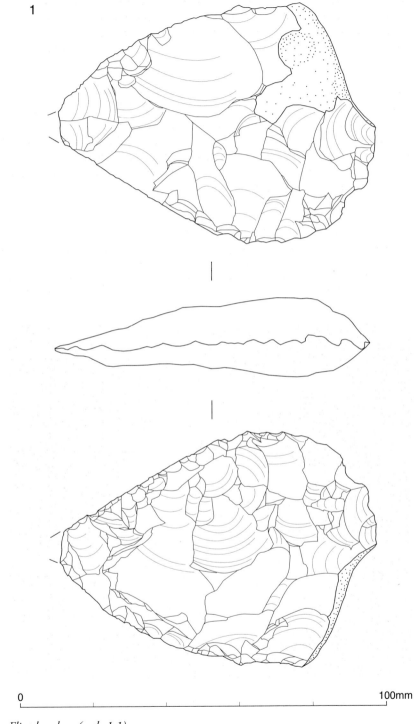

Fig. 14: Flint handaxe (scale 1:1)

the Lincolnshire Wolds (Roger Jacobi, pers. comm.) almost certainly derives from the natural glacial gravels. The colouring and quality of the remainder suggests that most material derives from non-local sources. Patination, where present, is light and seemingly confined to Mesolithic or older pieces. A single blade of probable Mesolithic date is more deeply altered to an all over white.

Palaeolithic (*incorporating information provided by Roger Jacobi*)

A single cordiform handaxe was recovered as an unstratified find from the central west area of the site (Figs 14–15). In isolation, this piece is not dateable, with the form essentially unchanged from throughout the Lower and Middle Palaeolithic. The sharp condition and light patina are noteworthy and suggest the handaxe itself had not been incorporated within a gravel deposit. This, together with a certain asymmetry in its working are possible indicators of this being a 'late' handaxe of Mousterian affinity, and therefore dating to the Middle Palaeolithic.

Catalogue of illustrated Palaeolithic worked flint (Fig. 14)

1   Small, cordiform handaxe. Sharp condition, light bluish yellow patina. Slight damage to tip. Raw material is cobble of yellow brown flint or fine-grained chert, probably from river gravel. Longer edges are convex and smooth. Flake scars more numerous on dorsal surface and with secondary fine retouch to edges and longitudinal tranchet scar to tip. Length 86mm; width 65mm; thickness 21mm. Unstratified.

Fig. 15:   Photograph of the flint handaxe (scale 1:1)

Mesolithic

Thirteen pieces, all of which are clearly re-deposited, are dateable to the Mesolithic period (Table 2). Blades and bladelets, most of which are broken, are well formed, with parallel edges and in some instances with platform abrasion. Utilised pieces (Fig. 16, nos 2 and 3) consist of a burin and a bladelet core fragment, which has been adapted for use as a scraper. The former is regarded as Mesolithic in this instance although it should be noted that burins also occur in Upper Palaeolithic and (more rarely) in Neolithic assemblages.

Catalogue of illustrated Mesolithic worked flint (Fig. 16)

2   Scraper on bladelet core fragment. Single-platform core with signs of platform abrasion. Grey flint with light, mottled patina. Abrupt retouch to one edge (under patina). Length 42mm. Unstratified.
3   Burin on blade-like flake. ?Broken at proximal end, rolled. Unpatinated grey flint. Spall from distal end. Partial abrupt or semi-abrupt retouch to longer edges. Length 65mm. Fill 2106 of ditch 2105, Period 2.

Bronze Age

The larger part of the worked flint assemblage exhibits characteristics consistent with flintworking from the Late Neolithic and Bronze Age periods (Fig. 16). Most abundant (Table 2) are flake removals, which tend towards broad, squat proportions. Striking platforms are unprepared, broad and frequently pronounced bulbs indicate use of hard-hammer percussion. Two flake cores/core fragments are of multi-platform type, all well reduced and displaying no signs of platform preparation or rejuvenation. The absence of tool types of Neolithic or Neolithic/Early Bronze Age date and the generally 'uncontrolled' appearance of some removals may indicate Middle or possibly later Bronze Age dating. The pieces with secondary working, including scrapers and piercers described below, all might reasonably be considered to date to the Late Neolithic to Early/Middle Bronze Age.

A small group of worked flint was recovered from Period 1 horizons (Table 2) and might potentially be regarded as stratified. This included a single tool, a piercer of likely Early to Middle Bronze Age date (Fig. 16, no. 4). Two small groups of debitage (each of three waste flakes) from Period 1 tree-throw pit 1063, fill 1064 and the primary fill, 1315, of Ditch 1, are notable for their fresh condition, perhaps indicating deposition not long following manufacture. Two flakes from Ditch 1 almost certainly derive from the same distinctively granular grey flint.

Catalogue of illustrated Bronze Age worked flint (Fig. 16)

4   Unpatinated dark grey-brown flint. Tip missing. Piercer/borer on hard-hammer-struck flake. Fine abrupt retouch to distal end. Length 31mm. Surface find from Ditch 1, Period 1.
5   Unpatinated grey flint. Unpatinated dark grey flint. Discoidal scraper on hard-hammer-struck flake. Continuous (to butt), abrupt retouch. Length 35mm. Unstratified.
6   Unpatinated dark grey flint. Extended endscraper on hard-hammer-struck flake. Partial, abrupt retouch. Length 41mm. Unstratified.

Discussion

This small group of lithics is most notable for its inclusion of a Palaeolithic handaxe, one of very few from Gloucestershire, particularly away from the Thames gravels in the south-east (Darvill 1987, 17–22). The condition of this item, while not conclusive as evidence of Mousterian (Middle Palaeolithic) dating, is evidence against its derivation from a gravel substrate, either local or further afield (see *Discussion*, below). Probable Mousterian axes are known from only two other findspots in the county, from Barnwood, Gloucester (Clifford

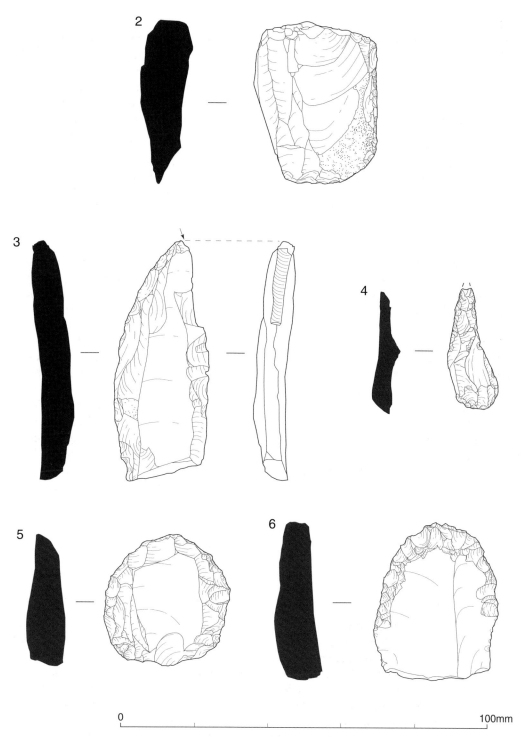

Fig. 16: Worked flint (scale 1:1)

1936, 91) and Lechlade (Clifford 1939, 193). On the other hand, the handaxe might have been incorporated into the gravel substrate if it had been deposited by hunter-gatherers exploiting the putative proglacial lake which is believed to have existed in the vicinity of the site (Darvill 2006, 14).

Burnt flint and stone, by E.R. McSloy

A large quantity of burnt stone was recovered, primarily from Period 1 contexts and concentrated in a small number of features. A proportion of this material (2.9kg) was recovered from soil samples, the remainder was hand collected during excavation but does not represent a full recovery of the material present on site. The bulk of the burnt stone of this material comprises frequently highly fragmented pebble or cobble-sized quartz or quartzite clasts of probable Triassic derivation and locally available. Use as heated stones probably for heating food ('pot-boilers') is most likely.

Burnt flint is far less abundant compared to the burnt stone, though similarly is concentrated in Period 1 contexts (Table 3). All was recovered from soil samples and consists of small fragments, almost certainly from the local gravels. The majority of this material appears fire-reddened rather than fully calcined. The likelihood is that this material derives from unintentional/non-selective processes such as hearths or fire-setting.

Table 3: Quantification by weight (g) of burnt stone and burnt flint by period

* = undated

	Period				
Category	1	2	3	5*	Total
Burnt flint	335	14	164	12	525
Burnt stone	6863	219	1693	1293	10068

Worked stone, by Fiona Roe

A single worked stone item was recovered from Period 4 (post-medieval) fill 2156 (Ditch 1130, not illustrated). This is a rotary quern fragment of Old Red Sandstone from the Forest of Dean region and is of Romano-British date. Romano-British querns made from Old Red Sandstone are common finds in Gloucestershire and were distributed far to the east (Shaffrey 2003).

The pottery, by E.R. McSloy

Pottery of all periods amounts to 1069 sherds (11.4kg). Small groups of Bronze Age and Romano-British material were recovered (Tables 4 and 5), with most dating to the medieval period, largely between the 11th and 13th/earlier 14th centuries.

Pottery fabrics were identified macroscopically or with the use of a (x4) hand lens. Represented fabrics are presented below, grouped according to the main inclusion type, which may reflect source and in the case of some Romano-British fabrics, firing characteristics. The coding scheme for medieval pottery follows that utilised for comparable material from Tinker's Close, Moreton-in-Marsh (Timby 2000, 20–1). Where applicable, fabrics have been matched against the Gloucester pottery type series (summarised in Vince 1983) and the *National Romano-British Fabric Reference Collection* (Tomber and Dore 1998). Quantification was by sherd count and weight for each fabric type by context. Estimated vessel equivalents (EVEs) were recorded for each identified vessel form. In addition, minimum number of vessels and sherd thicknesses were recorded for the prehistoric assemblage.

The condition of the pottery was extremely variable. Fabrics with calcareous inclusions are poorly preserved, particularly prehistoric fabrics F1 and F5, where leaching of inclusions has resulted in friable and fragile sherds and significant loss of surfaces. Grogged and flint-tempered fabrics among the prehistoric group are well preserved and average sherd weight (for all prehistoric pottery) is moderately high at 9.9g. The condition of the Romano-British group is poor with many sherds small and surface preservation very poor. Average sherd weight (with amphora sherds omitted) is moderately low for a Romano-British group at 10.6g. Elements of the medieval assemblage are well preserved, however some material is heavily fragmented and average sherd weight low at 9.4g.

Period 1: Bronze Age

Fifty-four sherds (532g) of prehistoric pottery representing a minimum of 27 vessels were recovered from 18 contexts. Dating of this material was rendered extremely difficult by the small quantities within each context, poor preservation of some material, and the paucity of diagnostic featured sherds. Radiocarbon determinations confirm the Middle Bronze Age dating suspected for pottery associated with the CPBSs and from Ditch 1, which comprised thick-walled sherds in (leached) calcareous-tempered and grogged fabrics. The remaining pottery, which is of different character and considered to be of later date, was associated with clusters of features to the north-west of Ditch 1.

Bronze Age fabrics

SHELL (SH)

SH1: Leached coarse shell. Handmade. Reddish-brown or buff-brown exterior surface and margin, dark grey interior surface and margin. Fabric is soft with a soapy feel and laminated fracture. Abundant plate-like voids, 1–5mm, resulting in a vesicular 'corky' appearance. Rare, well-sorted fine colourless or milky-white quartz (0.3mm). *Forms: thick-walled sherds (10–13mm); ?biconical urn.*

SH2: sparse shell/organic. Handmade. Reddish-brown exterior surface and dark grey interior surface and core. Fabric is soft with a smooth feel and finely irregular. Rare plate-like voids, 1–2mm probably representing leached fossil shell or possibly organic inclusions. Otherwise fabric is dense and inclusion free. *Forms: thin-walled sherds (6–7mm).*

GROG (GR)

GR1: coarse grog. Handmade. Buff-brown exterior surface and dark grey interior surface and core. Fabric is soft with a soapy feel and irregular/'lumpy'. Common, well-sorted, coarse (3–5mm), sub-rounded black, grog. *Forms: moderately thin-walled sherds (7–8mm); Flat-based vessels.*

GR2: fine grog/clay pellet with some leached shell. Handmade. Mid grey-brown throughout. Fabric is soft with a soapy feel and finely irregular fracture. Common, well-sorted, fine (0.5–1mm), sub-rounded, pale grey or buff-coloured clay pellet. Rare plate-like and rounded voids from leached calcareous inclusions. *Forms: 1 x thin-walled sherd (7–8mm).*

SANDY (Q)

Q1: sandy with quartzite. Handmade. Dark grey throughout or with reddish-brown exterior surface. Fabric is hard with a smooth feel and finely irregular fracture. Common medium (0.3–0.5mm) quartz sand and common/rare, well-sorted, coarse (1–4mm), sub-angular, white or pinkish quartzite. *Forms: thin-walled sherds (6–7mm); bipartite and globular vessels.*

Middle Bronze Age (Ditch 1 and CPBSs)

A total of 31 sherds (307g), representing a minimum of 13 vessels, is considered to be of Middle Bronze Age date. Pottery of this type derived predominantly from the fills of postholes associated with the CPBSs, with smaller quantities from layer deposit 1525 and Ditch 1 (Table 4).

Table 4: Prehistoric pottery by fabric (minimum no. of vessels and weight (g)) and location

Location	Fabric									
	GR1		GR2		Q1		SH1		SH2	
	Vess.	Wt.	Vess.	Wt.	Vess.	Wt.	Vess.	Wt.	Vess.	Wt.
Ditch 1	2	91	-	-	-	-	1	6	1	6
CPBSs	-	-	1	4	-	-	6	100	-	-
Layer 1525	-	-	-	-	-	-	1	1	-	-
Pit Group 2	-	-	-	-	6	127	-	-	-	-
Pit Group 3	-	-	-	-	-	-	1	1	4	46
Tree-throw pit 1248	-	-	-	-	-	-	2	38	1	13
Unstratified	1	99	-	-	-	-	-	-	-	-
Total	**3**	**190**	**1**	**4**	**6**	**127**	**11**	**146**	**6**	**65**

Pottery from the CPBSs almost exclusively comprised poorly preserved sherds belonging to vesicular fabric SH1 (Table 4). The majority are thick-walled sherds (in range 10–12mm), most probably deriving from large biconical or bucket/barrel urn-type vessels. A single rimsherd of expanded/T-shaped form was recovered from posthole 1072. This vessel also featured an applied strip with fingertip ornament below its rim (Fig. 17, no. 1). A second sherd from this context, almost certainly a biconical vessel (Fig. 17, no. 2), also featured an applied strip to its shoulder carination. Sherds from the remaining postholes were featureless with the exception of a small bodysherd from posthole 1072 (not illustrated) which exhibited part of a probable applied cordon.

The similarities in fabric of sherds from the CPBSs suggests all the material is of comparable date. Closest regional parallels are from among the cinerary group from Bevan's Quarry, Temple Guiting (O'Neil 1967, fig. 3). This group, the largest in the region, comprises mainly biconical form vessels with decorative elements, such as the applied, thumbed strips comparable to the southern English Deverel-Rimbury tradition.

Pottery from Ditch 1 was restricted to sherds from three vessels. A thick-walled sherd in a vesicular fabric is comparable to the group from the CPBSs. The remaining vessels, including the lower portion and base of a jar-like vessel (Fig. 17, no. 3) is of a grog-tempered fabric. The fabric of vessel no. 3 and absence of decoration (to its lower body) are characteristics appropriate for either Early Bronze Age (Collared Urn) or Middle Bronze Age 'urn' types.

Late Bronze Age/Late Bronze Age to Early Iron Age (Pit Groups 9 and 10 and pit 1248)

Pottery from features to the north of Ditch 1 amounted to 23 sherds (225g), representing 14 vessels. Sherds were thinner (6–8mm) compared to the Middle Bronze Age group and the range of fabrics quite distinct. Forms are restricted to a bipartite bowl (Fig. 17, no.

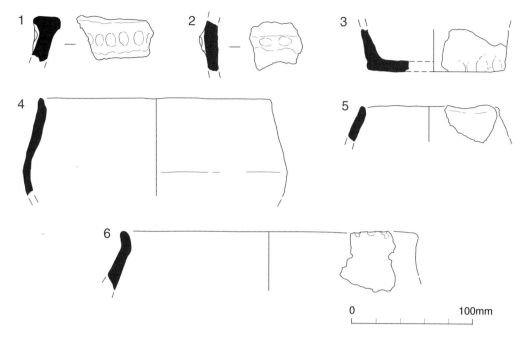

Fig. 17: Prehistoric pottery (scale 1:3)

4) and a ?globular vessel (Fig. 17, no. 6) with fingertip decoration to the rim. These are perhaps best paralleled among Late Bronze Age assemblages from southern and eastern Britain (Barrett 1980, 297–319). A later date, extending as late as the 6th/5th centuries BC, cannot be discounted.

Discussion

Pottery of Middle and Late Bronze Age date is scarce in north Gloucestershire and bordering counties (Evans 1990, 30; Woodward 1998, 63) and this meagre group is of some significance, occurring as it does in association with (probable) domestic structures. Comparable small groups of Middle Bronze Age pottery are known in northern Gloucestershire from Birdlip (Woodward 1998, 66–7) and Hucclecote (Clifford 1933, 332; Timby 2003, 31–6). A larger, cinerary, group is that from Bevan's Quarry, Temple Guiting (O'Neil 1967) where biconical urns and some bowl forms occur. The evidence suggests a regional tradition of biconical urns, vessel forms with an Earlier Bronze Age ancestry, and analogous in this respect to material from the Thames valley (Ellison 1984). Some elements such as use of impressed (fingernail?) decoration, recorded on sherds from Bevan's Quarry (O'Neil 1967, fig. 3, no. 3), Birdlip (Woodward 1998, fig. 26, no. 3) and the current site (Fig. 17, no. 1) may also be a local characteristic and representative of survival of an earlier tradition. Fabrics among the Middle Bronze Age group at Blenheim Farm are broadly comparable to those from other sites in the region. Not present were examples with igneous/metamorphic rock inclusions previously identified from Tewkesbury (Timby 2004, 59–62), where a Malverns source is likely, or as at Hucclecote (Vince 2003) where a more distant Derbyshire source was thought possible.

Material from features located to the north of Ditch 1 clearly belongs to a separate tradition and it is tempting to see this as representing continuity of activity into the Later Bronze Age. The appearance of sandy fabrics among this later group is significant, as they are also present in Late Bronze Age groups from Kemerton, Worcestershire (Evans 1990; Woodward 1998).

Catalogue of illustrated Bronze Age sherds (Fig. 17)

1   Expanded/T-shaped rim with applied, finger-tipped strip below. Fabric SH1. Fill 1073 of posthole 1072, CPBS1, Period 1.
2   Sherd with applied, finger-tipped strip. Fabric SH1. Fill 1073 of posthole 1072, CPBS1, Period 1.
3   Plain base. Fabric GR1. Fill 1371 of Ditch 1, Period 1.
4   Bipartite bowl with slightly out-curled plain rim. Fabric Q1. Fill 1137 of pit 1136, Pit Group 9, Period 1.
5   Bowl or jar with irregular, ?slightly everted rim. Fabric Q1. Fill 1328 of pit 1327, Pit Group 9, Period 1.
6   Bowl or jar with slightly out-curled plain rim with fingernail notches to rim outer. Fabric SH1. Tree-throw pit fill 1249, Period 1.

Period 2: Romano-British

Forty-nine sherds (1491g) of Romano-British pottery were recovered from 34 separate contexts, notably from the fills of Enclosures 1 and 2. A significant proportion, 28%, is residual, in medieval or later features.

Romano-British material is listed by fabric type in Table 5. Typically for Gloucestershire, the majority consists of Severn Valley ware, most likely originating from the Gloucester area or the Malvern Chase, together with small quantities from outside the region. Elements within the group including a Drag. 18/31 samian dish, a Savernake ware jar and a sherd of organic-tempered Severn Valley ware are indicative of earlier Romano-British, probably 2nd-century AD, dating. Little else can be said as to the wider significance of the group: the small quantities of material and its poor condition suggest that the focus for Romano-British settlement lies away from the excavated area.

Period 3: Medieval

Pottery of medieval date amounts to 948 sherds (9195g). Medieval fabrics can for the most part be matched to types published elsewhere and are described only briefly below.

Medieval fabrics

MALV
Unglazed Malvernian coarsewares. Gloucester fabric TF40 (Vince 1977; 1983, 130). Date range: 12th to 14th centuries. *Forms: straight-sided, everted-rim jars.*

MALVG/MALVO
Glazed Malvernian wares. Gloucester fabric TF52 (Vince 1983, 130). Date range: 13th to 16th centuries. A distinction is made here between the earlier, coarser fabric and later material characterised by fewer inclusions and firing to a universal pale orange. *Forms: bodysherd only.*

BRIL
Brill/Boarstall (Buckinghamshire) glazed ware. Oxfordshire fabric OXAM (Mellor 1994, 111–40). Date range: mid 13th to 14th centuries. *Forms: jugs.*

WARKW
Warwickshire whiteware. Worcestershire fabric 64.2. Date range: 13th to early 14th centuries. *Forms: wheel-thrown jars.*

Table 5: Quantification of Roman, medieval and post-medieval pottery by fabric

Fabric code	Description	Count	Weight (g)	EVEs
Roman				
BAT AM	Baetican amphora	1	985	-
DOR BB1	Dorset Black-Burnished ware	4	19	.04
LOC BS	Local black sandy coarseware	5	18	-
LOC GW	Local greyware	25	169	.12
LEZ SA	Central Gaulish (Lezoux) samian	2	55	-
SAV GT	Savernake ware	1	17	-
SVW OX2	Severn Valley oxidised	11	228	.24
Sub-total		*49*	*1491*	*.40*
Medieval				
MALV	Malvernian unglazed	49	595	.35
MALVG	Malvernian glazed	3	8	-
MALVO	Malvernian redware	8	174	.10
BRIL	Brill/Boarstall glazed	21	363	-
WARKW	Warwickshire buff sandy	52	873	.22
WARKG	Warwickshire buff sandy (glazed)	23	634	.62
FLIN	Flint-tempered	1	19	.06
MINT	Minety ware	48	556	.29
COTS	Cotswold oolitic	239	2521	2.65
WINCH	Cotswold oolitic with quartz	35	411	.15
SAND	?Worcester sandy wares	457	2812	1.34
GREY	Sandy wares (grey-firing)	9	165	.15
SAND GL	?Worcester sandy (glazed)	1	11	-
MISC WH	Misc glazed whiteware	2	53	.20
Sub-total		*948*	*9195*	*6.13*
Post-medieval				
	Black-glazed	4	32	-
	Misc. glazed red earthenware	8	134	-
	White salt-glazed stoneware	1	23	-
	Staffs yellow slipware	1	3	-
	Refined whiteware (china)	4	12	-
Sub-total		*18*	*204*	*-*
Total		**1015**	**10881**	**6.53**

WARKG

Warwickshire whiteware (glazed). Gloucester fabric TF102 (Vince 1983, 130). Worcestershire fabric 64.3. Production of similar material known at Chilver's Coton, Nuneaton. Date range: 13th to early 14th centuries. *Forms: highly decorated wheel-thrown jugs.*

FLINT

Unsourced cooking pot fabric characterised by rare coarse flint inclusions and leached limestone. Possibly from area of Kennet Valley ('Newbury B type').

MINT
Minety type (north Wiltshire) glazed, limestone-tempered ware. Gloucester fabric TF44 (Vince 1983, 130) Oxfordshire fabric OXBB (Mellor 1994, 111–40). Date range: 12th to 15th centuries. *Forms: jugs, jars/?pitchers.*

COTS
Oolitic limestone-tempered coarseware. Gloucester fabric TF41B (Vince 1983, 125); Oxfordshire fabric OXAC (Mellor 1994, 44). Date range: 11th to 13th centuries. *Forms: clubbed-rim jars; everted-rim jars; ?'west-country vessel'.*

WINCH
Variant of oolitic limestone-tempered coarseware with quartz sand. First identified at Winchcombe (Vince 1984, 263). Date range: 11th to ?13th centuries. *Forms: everted-rim jars.*

SAND
Unsourced sandy coarseware. Dark grey or black firing with abundant quartz. Affinities with Worcester type 55/Gloucester fabric TF91 (Vince 1983, 126). Might also derive from one or more south Warwickshire sources. Date range: 12th to mid 14th centuries. *Forms: straight-sided, everted-rim jars.*

GREY
Warwickshire grey-firing sandy coarseware. Probably corresponds to fabric 26A (Rátkai 1994, 98), common in Warwickshire and likely to be a local type. Date range: 13th to early 14th centuries. *Forms: jars with short, 'lid-seated' everted rims.*

SAND GL
Probably Worcester jug fabric (Bryant and Evans 2004, 290–1). Handmade. *Forms: bodysherd only.*

MISC WH
Unsourced white-firing fabric with sparse, thin pale-green glaze. Possibly (Hampshire/Surrey) Borderware. *Forms: Squared rim from probable jug.*

Assemblage composition

The pottery dates broadly to between the 11th and 13th/earlier 14th centuries, with perhaps the larger part to the later 12th and 13th centuries. Material dateable to after *c.* 1350 is present only as occasional sherds of Malvernian red ware and possible late Brill products. Relative dating was hindered by generally low numbers of sherds within each context and by the long-lived nature of many of the wares represented. Where specific chronological indicators assist with site phasing, these are described in the *Excavation Results*, above.

The medieval assemblage is quantified according to fabric in Tables 5–7. Pottery from Building 1 and its environs constitutes approximately one third of the whole medieval assemblage by sherd count, and is presented separately (Table 7). This group is distinct in terms of its fabric composition and considered to date to the period after *c.* 1260/75.

The assemblage is dominated by coarseware types: oolitic limestone-tempered fabrics COTS or variant type WINCH, and sandy wares type SAND (Tables 5–7). The oolitic-tempered groups exhibit greater variance in form. Jars predominate, either straight-sided with 'clubbed' or bead-like rims (Fig. 18, nos 7–10) or more globular with simple everted rims (Fig. 18, nos 11–12). Forms compare to examples from Whittington Court (Jope 1952, fig. 6, nos 1–6) and Gloucester Castle (Greatorex 1988, fig. 12, no. 2), as well as from Tinker's Close, Moreton-in-Marsh (Timby 2000, 20–1). The simple everted, flat and clubbed rims probably indicate dating, at least for elements of this material, to the 11th to mid 12th century. Similar dating is conjectured for a jar with stamped decoration (Fig. 18, no. 12). The form of the stamp is unusual, although a variety of different stamped designs are known with oolitic limestone-tempered wares of the same tradition from Oxfordshire (Mellor 1994, fig. 13, nos 20–5). Stamped material from Droitwich (Hurst 1992, fig. 95, nos 2–6) and from Bristol (Watts and Rahtz 1985, fig. 79, nos 59–66) is dated to the 11th

Table 6: Period 3 pottery, Building 1 omitted

Fabric	Count	%Count	Weight (g)	%Weight	EVEs
SAND	276	43.1	1571	26	.96
GREY	2	0.3	15	0.3	-
SAND GL	1	0.1	11	0.2	-
COTS	203	32.0	2139	35.8	2.28
WINCH	26	4.1	243	4.1	.05
WARKW	48	7.5	803	13.4	.12
MALV	19	3.0	271	4.5	.13
MALVG	2	0.3	4	0.1	-
MALVO	8	1.3	174	2.9	.10
WARKG	3	0.5	58	1.0	-
MINT	32	5.0	412	6.9	.29
BRIL	16	2.5	239	4.0	-
MISC WH	2	0.3	53	0.9	.20
Total	**636**		**5978**		**4.13**

Table 7: Period 3 pottery associated with Building 1

Fabric	Count	%Count	Weight (g)	%Weight	EVEs
SAND	160	57.8	1123	40	.34
GREY	7	2.5	150	5.3	.15
COTS	32	11.6	279	9.9	.27
WINCH	6	2.2	100	3.5	-
WARKW	3	1.1	62	2.2	.10
MALV	30	10.8	324	11.5	.22
WARKG	20	7.2	576	20.4	.62
MINT	16	5.8	144	5.1	-
BRIL	2	0.8	56	2.0	-
MALVG	1	0.4	4	0.1	-
Total	**277**		**2818**		**1.7**

and 12th centuries. Twelfth-century dating is likely for an inturned dish (Fig. 18, no. 13), a vessel form which exhibits a marked 'west country' distribution (Jope 1952, 65).

Sources for the sandy coarseware fabrics SAND, GREY and WARKW are unclear, although the resemblance of the latter to glazed fabric WARKG makes a Midlands origin likely for this type at least. For the reduced material the fabric and range of forms is comparable to material known to be produced at Worcester between the 12th and early 14th centuries (Morris 1980), however a closer source, perhaps in south Warwickshire is a possibility. Coarse sandy wares are known to be produced at Alcester (Cracknell and Jones 1985, 110–16), probably in the 12th and 13th centuries, and similar material forms a major component within medieval assemblages at Warwick (Rátkai 1988, 36–7). Represented forms in this fabric are restricted to jars, all of which are wheel-thrown or finished and feature 'developed' everted-rim types (Fig. 18, nos 14–18).

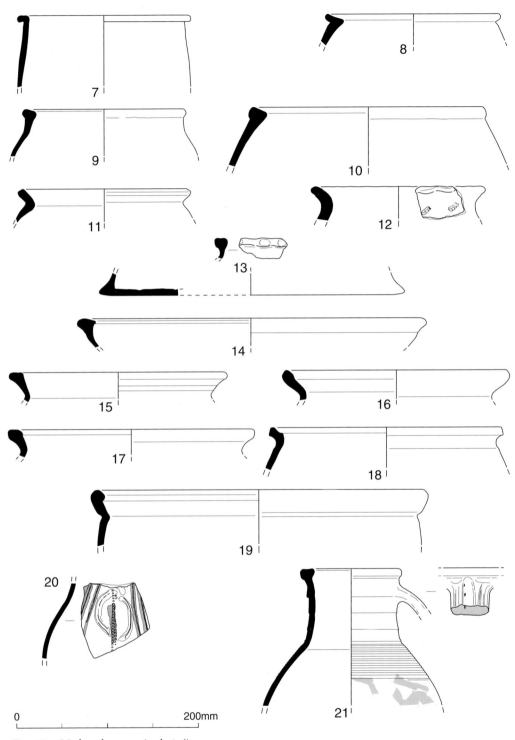

Fig. 18:   Medieval pottery (scale 1:4)

The Malvernian industry is poorly represented overall. Significantly its products are notice-ably more abundant in the Building 1 group (Table 7) and it may be that use of Malvernian cooking pots increases at a time coincident with the fall off in use of limestone-tempered fabrics, which are correspondingly less well represented in this group than on the remainder of the site. Forms consist of straight-sided jars with wheel-finished moulded everted rims, which probably date to the 13th century.

The location of Moreton-in-Marsh may be instrumental in the presence of tablewares from a number of contemporary sources, with no one type especially dominant. Minety ware, from north Wiltshire, occurs relatively consistently throughout the assemblage, probably reflecting the type's longevity throughout the period represented. Few forms were identifiable but significantly these include pitchers with combed wavy decoration representative of the earlier phases of production (before *c.* 1250) and later medieval vessel types (probably 14th to 15th century) including wheel-thrown jars and a rod-like, slashed jug handle. Brill/Boarstall material includes highly decorated jugs (Fig. 18, no. 20), of the type most prevalent in the middle years of the 13th century (Mellor 1994, 117), although this fabric is poorly represented in the Building 1 group.

There are clear similarities between glazed fabric WARKG and 'Midlands whiteware' fabric, a production site for which is known at Chilvers Cotton, Nuneaton (Ford 1995, 33–5). Nuneaton products are present among medieval assemblage in Gloucester (Vince 1983) where most are considered to date to the late 13th century. A similar date seems likely at Blenheim Farm where most sherds derive from the Building 1 group (Table 7). The group includes a large jug with distinctive neck rilling (Fig. 18, no. 21), a characteristic of this ware occurring at Midlands sites including Stafford (Ford 1995, fig. 15, no. 100) and Warwick (Rátkai 1988, fig. 18, no. 130).

Discussion

The medieval assemblage differs in a number of respects to the only other published group from the area, at Tinker's Close, Moreton-in-Marsh (Timby 2000, 18–21). While some of the earliest elements from Period 3, those containing Cotswold fabrics and including 'clubbed' cooking-pot rims, demonstrate some chronological overlap with the Tinker's Close assemblage, differences in the overall composition, best demonstrated by the Building 1 group, suggest that the larger part of the assemblage is of somewhat later date. The Building 1 group, on the basis of the glazed jug types present, is considered to date to between *c.* 1260/75 and *c.* 1350.

Sources for the ware types present indicate that coarsewares were acquired from various sources belonging to differing potting traditions. Some types, most notably Malvernian and Minety type wares, which were absent at Tinker's Close, occur at Blenheim Farm and suggest that compositional differences relate to chronology. There is good evidence, from the Building 1 group, for the declining importance of Cotswold limestone-tempered wares by the mid/late 13th century. Glazed tablewares dateable no earlier than the mid 13th century, such as Brill/Boarstall and Midlands whitewares, demonstrate access to increas-ingly diverse markets by the later medieval period.

Catalogue of illustrated medieval sherds (Fig. 18)

7   Jar with flat rim. Fabric COTS. Ditch fill 1561, Period 3b.
8   Jar with flat rim. Fabric COTS. Pit fill 2026, Period 3b.
9   Necked jar with clubbed rim. Fabric COTS. Fill 2564 of Paddock 5/6 ditch, Period 3a.

10 Jar with clubbed rim. Fabric COTS. Fill 1422 from Pit Group 120, Period 3a.
11 Jar with simple everted rim. Fabric COTS. Fill 2420 of Ditch Group 48, Period 3b.
12 Jar with simple everted rim and stamped decoration. Fabric COTS. Rubble layer 2208, Building 1, Period 3b.
13 Rim and base from inturned dish/'west country vessel'. Fabric COTS. Fill 2491 of Waterhole 1, Period 3b.
14 ?Bowl. Fabric SAND. Construction layer 2220 of Building 1, Period 3b.
15 Jar with 'developed' everted rim. Fabric SAND. Fill of 2229 of Building 1, Period 3b.
16 Jar with 'developed' everted rim. Fabric SAND. Rubble layer 2208 from Building 1, Period 3b.
17 Jar with 'developed' everted rim. Fabric SAND. Rubble layer 2208 from Building 1, Period 3b.
18 Jar with 'developed' everted rim. Fabric GREY. Fill of 2229 from Building 1, Period 3b.
19 Jar with 'developed' everted rim. Fabric MALV. Rubble layer 2215 from Building 1, Period 3b.
20 Jug with applied decoration. Fabric BRIL. Rubble layer 2215 from Building 1, Period 3b.
21 Jug with rilling and painted/slipped decoration. Fabric WARKG. Rubble layer 2215 from Building 1, Period 3b.

Metalwork, by E.R. McSloy

Seven items of iron were recovered. All derive from medieval contexts and comprise nail fragments, a knife and a possible angle tie. Whittle tang knife no. 1 is the only item possible to date by form, if only broadly. The blade form is known elsewhere from 12th to 15th-century contexts (Goodall 1980, 81–2), although it is most likely to date to the late 13th to 14th centuries (Cowgill *et al.* 1987, 80–6).

Non-illustrated metal artefacts

Iron whittle-tang knife. X-radiography indicates the presence of a welded-on cutting edge, probably of steel. Tapering triangular blade with straight back and cutting edge and rounded tip. Tang central to blade. Length 134mm; width (at shoulder) 22mm. Step 2221, Building 1, Period 3b.

Metallurgical residues, by E.R. McSloy

A small quantity (989g) of metallurgical residue comprising miscellaneous ironworking slag was recovered (Table 8). Such material consists of formless, blocky material which might equally have been formed as the result of smithing or smelting processes. The bulk of material derives from Period 4 post-medieval contexts. Overall the small quantities of slag and the absence of micro-residues argue against metalworking activity in the near vicinity.

In addition to the ironworking slag, small quantities (13g) of fuel ash were recovered from Period 1 and Period 2 contexts, as well as 629g of 'fuel ash slag'. The formation of fuel ash slag is not directly related to metallurgical processes but may result from elevated temperatures and the reaction between alkaline fuel ash and silicates present in either clay or in sandy ground surfaces.

Table 8: metallurgical residues by weight (g) and Period

* = undated

	Period					
Type	1	2	3	4	5*	Total
Miscellaneous ironworking	-	21	203	525	240	989
Fuel ash	6	7	-	-	-	13

Leather, by Quita Mould

A single medieval shoe sole of turnshoe construction was recovered from Waterhole 2, fill 2486 (Fig. 13). The fill is undated though pottery from an associated fill is dated to the 12th to 13th century. As the shoe lacks its upper nothing can be said of the original style of the shoe, however, the broad shape of the sole suggests an early 13th-century date.

Non-illustrated leather artefacts

Leather turnshoe sole for the right foot. The sole is broad with a medium tread, wide but distinctly formed waist, and a wide seat. Edge/flesh seam with stitch length 6–7mm. The toe area is missing and the rest is heavily worn, with a circular hole worn in the centre of the tread and a large hole at the seat. Heavily worn tunnel stitching visible on grain side indicating that the sole had at least two clump repairs attached at the forepart and the seat. Six pieces of rand with an edge/flesh seam, maximum width 8mm. Sole length 245mm+. Width tread 98mm, waist 63mm, seat 77mm. Size adult 4+ (continental 37+). Fill 2486 of Waterhole 2, Period 3b.

THE BIOLOGICAL EVIDENCE

Human remains, by Teresa Gilmore

The material submitted for analysis was retrieved from 20 litres of a 30-litre environmental sample <1> (fill 1010, tree-throw pit 1008). The sample was sieved using a 2mm mesh. Analysis involved separating the cremated material into two fractions, >10mm and >2mm. Each fraction was weighed and the dimensions of the largest fragments were recorded. The dominant colour of the cremated material was noted along with any recognisable skeletal elements.

The amount of cremated bone present (146.8g) is not consistent with a complete adult cremation burial (which is typically in the range 1000.5g–2422.5g; McKinley 1993). All the identifiable fragments were adult and represented one individual.

The colour of the bone was white/light grey suggesting a temperature around 700–800°C and a high degree of oxidation during the cremation process. Only 9% of material was present in >10mm fraction compared to 89% in the >2mm fraction, suggesting high fragmentation, possibly due to raking of the pyre site (the remaining 2% was smaller than 2mm). Within the 10mm fraction eight fragments were recorded of which only one, a femoral distal epipcondyle (top of the knee) was identifiable. Within the 2mm fraction 50 fragments were recorded including two wormian bones, a frontal sinus, a cervical vertebra, the roots of a premolar and canine, and a distal manus phalange. The presence of small bones such as wormian and finger bones may also be indicative of raking to collect bone from the pyre site. Fragment weights and dimensions can be found in the site archive.

Animal bone, by Lorraine Higbee

A small number of animal bone fragments was recovered during hand excavation and from bulk soil samples processed by wet-sieving. The diagnostic fraction amounts to 35 fragments of which the majority derived from medieval and post-medieval contexts. The entire assemblage was subjected to assessment by rapidly scanning following Davis (1992).

The majority of fragments are moderately well preserved. The assemblage includes a small range of domestic species. Gnaw marks are rare and no butchery marks were observed, although this may be due to erosion of the bone surfaces.

A sheep/goat mandible was recovered from Period 1. Wear on the third molar suggested that it is from an animal aged at least 4–6 years (Payne 1973). Period 2 deposits yielded three loose horse teeth, all surface finds (context 1237) from Field System 1. Animal bone was recovered from 11 Period 3 contexts including layers and the fills of ditches. Cattle, sheep/goat, pig, horse and dog have all been identified. The bones identified include mandibles, loose teeth and/or metapodials. In Period 4, horse is the most common species by diagnostic fragment count. Of the other identified species, cattle bones are more abundant than sheep/goat and are represented by a wider range of skeletal elements than in the previous period, including long bones from both fore and hind limbs.

This small assemblage includes the main domestic species. The bias of elements present in favour of mandibles, teeth and metapodials is likely to be the result of the burial conditions. Most ageable specimens were subadult or adult. It is difficult to take the interpretation further with such a small assemblage.

Pollen, by Heather M. Tinsley

Two monoliths for pollen sampling were removed from a section across Ditch 1, although only the lower one, monolith 2, was examined for pollen (for location see Fig. 4). Subsamples for pollen analysis consisting of 5ml of sediment were removed with reference to the stratigraphic descriptions recorded. All samples were prepared using standard techniques (Moore *et al.* 1991). Plant nomenclature follows Stace (1991); pollen types generally follow Bennett (1994).

Very little pollen was recovered from any of the samples and the grains that were found were in a poor state of preservation. Two contexts, (primary) fill 1315 and fill 1316, produced no pollen although the latter contained single spores of undifferentiated Filicales (fern) and *Pteridium aquilinum* (bracken). Deposit 1048, a red-brown sandy slump on the outer side of the ditch, produced one grain of *Alnus* (alder) pollen. Layer 1317, an orange silty sand, contained the most pollen: 12 grains were recorded in 15 traverses of the slide, with 106 *Lycopodium* spores recovered. This very limited pollen assemblage consisted of four grains of *Alnus*, three of *Corylus*-type (hazel), two of *Quercus* (oak), two of Poaceae (grasses) and one grain of Lactuceae (dandelion and related Asteraceae). In addition, nine spores of Filicales were found along with single spores of *Pteridium aquilinum* and *Sphagnum* (bog moss). Deposit 1050 (the uppermost), a red-brown silty sand, contained two grains of *Alnus*, one of *Corylus*-type and of *Quercus*. The few pollen grains that were recovered from deposits 1050, 1317 and 1048 were all in a poor state of preservation, the exines of the grains were thin and structural features had been lost. This suggests corrosion caused by bacterial attack in the presence of air (Tipping 2000). The overall organic content of the sediments appeared to be very low. This suggests either that the fills accumulated rapidly without standstill phases during which vegetation colonised the ditch or, that if such phases did occur, later oxidation of organic matter has been more or less complete. The lack of recovery of pollen in these samples is not the result of a calcareous environment, the poor preservation is due to the ditch environment having been dry.

Charcoal, by Rowena Gale

Charcoal remains were extracted from the majority of samples taken, as well as from 16 hand-picked samples which included much larger fragments. The charcoal deposits were extremely sparse and frequently consisted of a few small specks of material. The condition of the charcoal varied from firm and well preserved to poor, friable and degraded. Some samples were vitrified (the result of exposure to temperatures exceeding 800°C). Standard methods were used to prepare the samples for examination (Gale and Cutler 2000). Where possible the maturity of the wood was assessed (i.e. heartwood/sapwood). Material suitable for radiocarbon dating was selected. The origin of the charcoal is unknown, although most of it probably originated from fuel debris.

Period 1: Middle/Late Bronze Age to Early Iron Age
Charcoal was recovered from CPBS 3 posthole 1473, fill 1474 (Figs 5 and 7, section 7) and Pit Group 12, pit 1860. Species identified included oak (*Quercus* sp.), hazel (*Corylus avellana*), blackthorn (*Prunus spinosa*), hawthorn/*Sorbus* group, willow (*Salix* sp.), poplar (*Populus* sp.) ash (*Fraxinus excelsior*) and alder (*Alnus glutinosa*). Hazel charcoal from CPBS3 posthole fill 1474 and Pit Group 12 pit fill 1861 were radiocarbon dated (see *The Radiocarbon Dates*, above). The fill, 1249, of tree-throw pit 1248 contained oak roundwood.

Period 2: Romano-British
Charcoal was extremely sparse from the fill of Enclosure 1 ditch recut 1250, and included very small fragments of blackthorn (*Prunus spinosa*), hawthorn/*Sorbus* group (*Pomoideae*), willow (*Salix* sp.) and poplar (*Populus* sp.). Field maple (*Acer campestre*) and alder (*Alnus glutinosa*) were recovered from the recut of Enclosure 2, ditch fill 2068.

Period 3: Medieval
Hazel (*Corylus avellana*), oak (*Quercus* sp.), blackthorn (*Prunus spinosa*), field maple (*Acer campestre*) and heather (*Ericacea*) were recovered from nine samples. The structure of the hazel roundwood in sample 70 from Pit Group 96 pit 1798, fill 1799, was consistent with that of coppice stems. Waterlogged wood from Waterhole 2 was recorded as narrow stems and thorns from blackthorn (*Prunus spinosa*).

Period 5: Undated
Undated material comprised species such as oak (*Quercus* sp.), blackthorn (*Prunus spinosa*), field maple (*Acer campestre*), hazel (*Corylus avellana*), holly *(Ilex aquifolium)* and the hawthorn/*Sorbus* group (*Pomoideae*).

Discussion
A relatively wide range of large woodland species were identified including oak (*Quercus* sp.), field maple (*Acer campestre*), ash (*Fraxinus excelsior*), holly (*Ilex aquifolium*) and hazel (*Corylus avellana*). These species would not have tolerated the typically wet or flooded soils that seem to have prevailed in the vicinity of the site, so wood/fuel must have been obtained from woodland on drier soils. If efforts were made to drain the land it is feasible that waste materials, such as hearth debris (charcoal), were dumped here to raise the ground level or to utilise low-grade farmland.

Marginal woodland or scrub included blackthorn and the hawthorn group (Pomoideae).

These species may have been grown as hedging. Hazel probably colonised open areas (as suggested by the presence of nutshell in the charcoal assemblage). Given the proximity of the site to a stream, it is interesting to note the low ratio of wetland species in the charcoal deposits, e.g. alder (*Alnus glutinosa*), willow (*Salix* sp.) and poplar (*Populus* sp.), which probably grew in abundance. As a potentially fast-regenerating wood resource these species may have been more important for other purposes, such as wattlework. The insect assemblage from Waterhole 2 included *Hylesinus crenatus,* which lives on ash (see *Insect remains,* below). The damp acid soils may also have encouraged the growth of heather and associated heathland species.

Oak and hazel were recorded in Middle/Late Bronze Age to Early Iron Age deposits and shrubby species (blackthorn, hawthorn) in the Romano-British period. It seems likely that mixed deciduous woodland, probably dominated by oak, grew within access of the site. The charcoal was mainly too comminuted to assess the possibility of managed woodland, although the character of hazel roundwood recovered was indicative of coppicing.

Charred and waterlogged plant remains, by Wendy Carruthers

Soil samples were taken from a range of deposits for environmental information and artefact recovery. Postholes, ditches, pits, middens, a hearth and waterholes were sampled and processed using standard methods of flotation. A 500-micron mesh was used to retain the flots and residues. Following the assessment recommendations (Carruthers 2005) further selected samples were processed. The results of the analysis are presented in Tables 9 and 10. Nomenclature and much of the habitat information follow Stace (1997). Cereal identifications follow Jacomet (1987). Ellenberg's indicator values were used to provide information about weed ecology (Hill *et al.* 1999). The limitations of the assemblage are noted in detail in the archive report.

Charred plant remains were recovered from a high proportion (88%) of the samples but preservation was generally very poor, with vacuolation, surface erosion and fragmentation. Modern fibrous roots and seeds were common in most of the samples. Concentrations of charred plant remains were low in the prehistoric samples with medieval samples more productive, particularly samples <70> from pit 1798 (Pit Group 96), <73> from Ditch 51, (Enclosure 5) and <81> from ditch 2312 (Paddocks 5/6), the latter producing over 200 fragments per litre. In addition, waterlogged plant remains were recovered from five samples, all from Hollow 2149 and Waterhole 2.

The poor state of preservation of the remains caused identification difficulties: bread wheat was positively identified in only four samples and cultivated vetches and peas (legumes) were not identified to species level unless the hilum was preserved, as the size ranges of the weed and cultivated taxa overlap. The presence of cultivated vetch was confirmed in the three richest samples, where better preservation produced a few seeds with hila. Celtic bean (*Vicia faba* var. *minor*) is usually easily recognised by its large size and oblong shape. The absence of hulled wheat from 27 of the samples is also noteworthy.

Charred plant material from three samples (<10>, <58> and <65>) was submitted for radiocarbon dating as some aspects of the charred plant assemblages were not typical of the prehistoric period (see *The Radiocarbon Dates,* above). The results confirmed that some of the charred plant material was intrusive, with the known contaminants dating to the medieval period. The source of this contamination is uncertain.

Period 1: Middle/Late Bronze Age to Early Iron Age

The concentrations of remains were low and very little cereal processing waste was recovered. The weed ecology is commonly recovered from charred assemblages of all periods. Wet or damp ground weeds such as sedges (*Carex* sp.) were present but infrequent. Stinking chamomile (*Anthemis cotula*) seeds were sparse in comparison with the medieval samples. This indicator of damp, heavy soils is mainly recovered from Iron Age and later sites, reflecting the expansion onto heavier clay soils that occurred in the later prehistoric period (Jones 1981).

Of the economic plants represented in the Bronze Age samples, the cereals most likely to be contemporary are the hulled wheats emmer and/or spelt (*Triticum dicoccum/spelta* and hulled barley (*Hordeum* sp.). It is uncertain whether any of the bread-type wheat, oats or rye were cultivated, although oats (radiocarbon dated to the Middle Bronze Age) were being grown on the acidic soils. The cultivated vetch seed (*Vicia sativa* ssp. *sativa*) from <47> (layer 1525) is most likely to be a contaminant, as this fodder crop has not been recovered from deposits earlier than the Anglo-Saxon period. The recovery of hazelnut shell fragments (*Corylus avellana*) from eight of the features, including a large number from <29> (pit 1331, Pit Group 9), indicates that wild foods such as fruits and nuts were still an important aspect of the diet.

Period 3: Medieval

Both waterlogged and charred plant remains were recovered from the 14 medieval samples (Table 10). In the case of Waterhole 2 the interpretation was enhanced by the examination of insect remains (see *Insect remains*, below). As is common for the 11th to 14th century, all four cereals known from this period were present: free-threshing wheat, hulled barley, oats and rye. Although chaff fragments were seldom preserved to determine precisely which species were being cultivated (e.g. *Avena* sp. = wild/cultivated oat), it is fairly clear from the quantities of grains recovered that all of these crops were important to the economy.

The three richest assemblages (<70>, <73> and <81>) are useful indicators for the medieval period. The proportions of grain recovered from these samples confirms the importance of all four main crops (Table 11). The grain:chaff:weed seed ratios were fairly similar suggesting they had been derived from similar activities. All were grain-rich with little chaff, as is typical of medieval assemblages. Although weed seeds were fairly frequent in all three samples, the deposits probably consisted of processed grain from a mixture of crops that had been grown under quite poor conditions (see below). The assemblages could represent grain burnt accidentally and cleaned out of drying ovens and hearths, or spoilt grain that was deliberately being destroyed.

The weed assemblages were dominated by small, light seeds such as stinking chamomile (*Anthemis cotula*) and scentless mayweed (*Tripleurospermum inodorum*). Large, heavy weed seeds such as corn cockle (*Agrostemma githago*) and black bindweed (*Fallopia convolvulus*) although not frequent were more common in the paddock ditches. Sample <81> was either better preserved or contained more waste from the earlier stages of processing.

Although free-threshing wheat was the dominant cereal in all three samples, oats were almost as frequent in sample <70> and rye was notably frequent in samples <70> and <81>. These cereals are often present in fairly low percentages on medieval sites, and it has been suggested that this is because these cereals were used primarily for fodder, and were less likely to become charred than bread (Wilkinson and Stevens 2003, 157).

The weed ecology suggests some of the soils were fairly impoverished as small-seeded

Table 9: Charred plant remains from Period 1 (prehistoric) features

Feature types: p = pit; d = ditch; ph = posthole; w = waterhole.
Feature Groups: CPBS = Circular Post-Built Structure; PG = Pit Group; W = Waterhole; D = Ditch
Habitat Preferences: A = arable; C = cultivated; D = disturbed/waste; E = heath; G = grassland; H = hedgerow; M = marsh/bog; R = rivers/ditches/ponds; S = scrub; W = woods; Y = waysides/hedgerows; a = acidic soils; c = calcareous soils; d = dry soils; h = heavy soils; n = nutrient-rich soils; o = open ground; w = wet/damp soils.
* = plant of economic value.
cf. = uncertain ID

	Common name	Habitat	Sample no: 1	2	8	9	10	23	27	29	37	38	41	43
			Context no: 1010	1073	1088	1096	1102	1322	1137	1332	1114	1115	1189	1352
			Feature: p1008	ph1072	ph1087	ph1095	ph1101	ph1321	ph1136	p1331	ph1116	ph1116	ph1206	ph1351
			Feature Group: -	CPBS1	CPBS1	CPBS1	CPBS1	PG 9	PG 9	PG 9	CPBS2	CPBS2	CPBS2	CPBS2
Cereals (grain):														
Triticum aestivum-type	bread-type free-threshing wheat		-	2	cf.4	cf.4	2	-	-	cf.1	-	cf.3	1	-
Triticum dicoccum/spelta	emmer/spelt wheat		-	-	-	-	3+	-	-	-	-	-	-	-
Triticum sp.	wheat		-	-	-	9	8	1	-	-	-	5	-	-
Barley NFI	barley		1	-	-	-	-	-	-	-	-	cf.2	1	1
Secale cereale L./*Triticum* sp.	rye/wheat		-	3	-	-	-	-	-	-	-	-	-	-
Avena/Bromus sp.	oat/chess		-	-	-	2	-	-	-	-	1	1	-	-
Indeterminate cereal grains			1	7	7	22	27	-	-	-	3	7	3	4
Chaff :														
Triticum dicoccum/spelta (glume base)	emmer/spelt wheat		-	-	-	-	-	-	1	-	-	-	-	-
Weeds :														
Corylus avellana L. (shell frag.)	hazelnut	HSW*	-	-	-	-	-	18	5	85	-	-	-	8
Fallopia convolvulus (L.) A.Love (achene)	black-bindweed	AD	3	-	-	-	-	-	-	-	-	-	-	-

40

Persicaria maculosa Gray (nutlet)	redshank	CDo	2	-	-	-	-	-	-	-	-	-	-	-
Rumex sp. (achene)	dock	CDG	-	1	-	1	-	-	-	-	-	-	-	-
Raphanus raphanistrum L. (capsule)	wild radish	CD	-	-	-	-	-	-	-	-	-	-	1fg	-
Vicia/Lathyrus sp. (<=2mm, small seeded)	weed vetch/tare	CDG	-	2	1	2	-	-	-	-	-	1	-	-
Vicia/Lathyrus sp. (3-4mm, small seeded)	weed vetch/tare	CDG	-	4	2	1	1	1	1	-	1	-	-	-
Vicia/Lathyrus/Pisum sp.	large legume		-	-	-	1	-	-	1	-	1	-	1	-
Anthemis cotula L. (achene)	stinking chamomile	ADhw	-	-	-	1	-	-	-	1	-	-	-	-
Odontites vernal/Euphrasia sp.	red bartsia/eyebright	CD	-	-	-	-	2	-	-	-	-	-	-	-
Galium aparine L.	cleavers	CDH	2	-	-	-	-	-	-	1	-	-	-	-
Sambucus nigra L. (seed)	elder	HSW*	1	-	-	-	-	-	-	-	-	-	-	-
Carex sp. (nutlet)	trigonous sedge	MPw	-	-	-	-	-	-	-	-	1	-	-	-
Bromus sect. *Bromus* (caryopsis)	chess	ADG	-	1	-	-	1	-	-	-	-	-	-	1
Poaceae *Poa*-type (caryopsis)	small seeded grass	CDG	-	-	1	-	-	-	-	-	-	-	-	-
		Total:	10	20	16	42	44	19	7	88	6	19	6	14
		Sample size:	40	30	20	20	20	10	10	40	10	20	10	10
		Fragments per litre:	0.25	0.7	0.8	2.1	2.2	1.9	0.7	2.2	0.6	1	0.6	1.4

41

Table 9: Charred plant remains from Period 1 (prehistoric) features (cntd)

		45	47	51	52	53	55	58	59	62	65	69
Sample no:		45	47	51	52	53	55	58	59	62	65	69
Context no:		1162	1525	1470	1472	1478	1464	1474	1476	1433	1861	1943
Feature:		w1158	layer	ph1469	ph1469	ph1477	ph1463	ph1473	ph1473	d1429	p1860	p1942
Feature Group:		W 1	-	CPBS3	CPBS3	CPBS3	CPBS3	CPBS3	CPBS3	D 1	PG 12	PG 134
Common name	**Habitat**											
Cereals (grain):												
Triticum aestivum-type — bread-type free-threshing wheat		-	22	cf.1	2fg	1	4	4	-	-	7	-
Triticum dicoccum/spelta — emmer/spelt wheat		-	-	-	-	-	-	-	-	cf.2	-	-
Triticum sp. — wheat		1	13	-	-	-	-	-	1	2	-	-
Hordeum sp. — barley		1	-	2	-	-	-	-	-	-	4	-
Triticum/Secale cereale — wheat/rye		-	-	-	-	-	-	-	-	2	-	-
Secale cereale L. / *Triticum* sp. — rye/wheat		cf.1	2cf.2	-	-	-	1	-	-	1	cf.1	-
Avena sp. — wild/cultivated oat		-	-	1	-	-	-	2+	-	-	9	-
Avena/Bromus sp. — oat/chess		-	2	-	-	-	-	-	-	-	1	-
Indeterminate cereal grains		1	66	5	-	5	5	1	6	-	12	6
Chaff :												
Triticum sp. (rachis frag.) — free-threshing wheat		-	2	-	-	-	-	-	-	-	-	-
Triticum dicoccum/spelta (glume base) — emmer/spelt wheat		-	-	1	-	-	-	-	-	-	-	-
Weeds :												
Corylus avellana L. (shell frag.) — hazelnut	HSW*	4	-	-	-	-	-	1+	-	1	-	-
Persicaria maculosa Gray (nutlet) — redshank	CDo	-	1	-	-	-	-	-	-	-	-	-
Rumex sp. (achene) — dock	CDG	-	4	-	-	-	-	-	-	-	-	-
Vicia sativa ssp. *sativa* — cultivated vetch	*	-	1	-	-	-	-	-	-	-	-	-
Vicia/Lathyrus sp. (<=2mm, small seeded) — weed vetch/tare	CDG	-	5	-	1	-	-	-	-	-	1	1

42

Species	Common name	Code											
Vicia/Lathyrus sp. (3-4mm, small seeded)	weed vetch/tare	CDG	–	1	1	1	1	1	–	2	–	–	1
Vicia/Lathyrus/Pisum sp.	large legume		2	–	–	–	–	–	1	–	–	–	–
Anthemis cotula L. (achene)	stinking chamomile	ADhw	–	1	–	1	–	1	–	–	–	–	2
Tripleurospermum inodorum (L.)Sch.Bip.	scentless mayweed	CD	–	1	–	–	–	–	–	–	–	–	–
Primulaceae	pimpernel etc.		–	1	–	–	–	–	–	–	–	–	–
Carex sp. (nutlet)	trigonous sedge	MPw	–	–	1	–	–	–	–	–	–	–	–
Bromus sect. *Bromus* (caryopsis)	chess	ADG	–	7	–	–	1	–	1	1	–	–	–
Danthonia decumbens (L.)DC (caryopsis)	heath-grass	psEG	–	cf.1	–	–	–	–	–	–	–	–	–
Poaceae *Lolium*-type (caryopsis)	*Lolium*-type grass	CDG	–	2	–	–	–	–	–	–	–	–	–
Total:			10	134	12	5	7	11	9	10	9	35	10
Sample size:			40	30	10	<10	<10	<10	<10	<10	<10	40	30
Fragments per litre:			0.25	4.5	1.2	0.5	0.7	1.1	0.9	1	0.3	0.9	0.33

43

Table 10: *Charred and waterlogged plant remains from Period 3 (medieval) features*

Sample no: † = number extrapolated from a count of 25% (<81>) or 50% (<73>) by volume
Feature types: p = pit; d =ditch; occu = occupation layer; h = hearth; demo = demolition layer; w = waterhole
Feature Groups: PG = Pit Group; Enc = Enclosure; Ho = Hollow; B = Building; P = Paddock; W = Waterhole.
Habitat Preferences: A = arable; C = cultivated; D = disturbed/waste; E = heath; G = grassland; H = hedgerow; M = marsh/bog; R = rivers/ditches/ponds; S = scrub; W = woods; Y = waysides/hedgerows; a = acidic soils; c = calcareous soils; d = dry soils; n = nutrient-rich soils; o = open ground; w = wet/damp soils. * = plant of economic value. [ ] = charred; no brackets = waterlogged. cf. = uncertain ID   h = some seeds still in fragments of seed head.

			64	67	70	73†	74	76	78	79	80	81†	82	83	84	85
Sample no:			64	67	70	73†	74	76	78	79	80	81†	82	83	84	85
Context no:			1758	1934	1799	2143	2134	2212	2235	2236	2229	2313	2486	2491	2506	2515
Feature type:			p1757	p1933	p1798	d51	d2132	occu h2223	h2223	occu demo	demo	d2312	w2502	w2502	w2502	w2502
Feature Group:			PG 93	PG 96	PG 96	Enc 5	Ho 2149	B 1	B 1	B 1	B 1	P 5/6	W 2	W 2	W 2	W 2
Species	Common name	Habitat														
Cereals (grain) and Legumes (seeds):																
Triticum aestivum/turgidum	bread/rivet-type free-threshing wheat	*	[10]	[5]	[318]	[1160]	-	[2]	[4]	[17]	[10]	[2760]	Cf.[1]	-	[2]	[1]
Triticum sp.	wheat	*	-	-	-	-	-	-	-	-	-	-	-	-	-	-
Hordeum sp.	barley	*	-	[1]	[86]	[220]	-	-	[2]	[8]	-	[216]	-	-	-	-
Secale cereale L.	rye	*	[3]	[3]	[159]	[52]	-	-	[2]	[4]	-	[1108]	-	[1]	-	[1]
Avena sp.	wild/cultivated oat	A*	-	-	[286]	[100]	-	-	[3]	[1]	-	[304]	[1]	-	-	-
Avena/Bromus sp.	oat/chess	A*	-	[4]	-	-	-	-	-	[5]	-	[256]	-	-	-	-
Indeterminate cereals	-	*	[8]	[19]	[541]	[1658]	-	[5]	[8]	[37]	[8]	[2620]	[1]	[4]	-	1 [2]
Pisum sativum L.	pea	*	cf.[3]	[1]	[1]cf.[9]	-	-	-	-	-	-	cf.[1]	-	-	-	-
Vicia faba var. minor	Celtic bean	*	[1]	-	[12]	-	-	-	-	-	-	[6]	-	-	-	-
Vicia/Lathyrus sp. (3-4mm seeded)	vetch/tare	CDG*	[6]	-	[47]	[100]	-	[1]	-	[1]	-	[26]	-	-	[2]	-
Vicia sativa ssp. sativa	cultivated vetch	-	-	-	[1]	[5]	-	-	-	-	-	[2]	-	-	-	-
Vicia/Lathyrus/Pisum (frag.)	vetch/tare/pea	-	[1]	-	[9]	-	-	-	[2]	-	-	[1]	-	-	-	-

Chaff:

Taxon		code							
Triticum turgidum-type (rachis frag.)	rivet-type wheat	*	[1]	-	-	-	-	cf.[2]	cf.[2]
T. aestivum-type (rachis frag.)	bread-type wheat	*	[7]	[1]	[1]	-	[1]	-	cf.[2]
Triticum sp. (rachis frag.)	free-threshing wheat	*	[51]	[4]	[47]	[2]	-	-	-
Hordeum (rachis frag.)	barley	*	[13]	[6]	[5]	-	[1]	-	-
Secale cereale L. (rachis frag.)	rye	*	[25]	[4]	[2]	-	-	-	-
Avena sp (awn frag.)	oat	A*	+	-	-	-	-	-	-
Avena fatua L. (floret base)	wild oat	A	[1]	-	-	-	-	-	-
Cereal-sized culm node	-	A*	[15]	[12]	[2]	[1]	-	-	-

Weeds etc:

Taxon		code							
Ranunculus repens/acris/bulbosus (achene)	buttercup	DG	12	[2]	99	16	3	3	-
R. subg. *Batrachium* (achene)	crowfoot	BP	1	-	-	11	3	6	-
R. flammula L. (achene)	lesser spearwort	MPGw	40	-	-	-	7	-	-
Chelidonium majus L. (seed)	greater celandine	HY	-	-	27	-	-	-	-
Urtica dioica L. (achene)	stinging nettle	CDn	1	-	20	-	1	1	-
U. urens L. (achene)	small nettle	CDn	3	[1]	-	-	6	-	-
Corylus avellana L. (shell frag.)	hazelnut	HSW*	-	[1]	-	-	-	-	-
Chenopodium album L.	fat hen	CDn	11	-	-	2	18	-	-
Atriplex patula/prostrate	orache	CDn	4	-	-	-	10	20	-
Montia fontana ssp. *chondrosperma*(Fenzl)Walters	blinks	PGw	59	-	-	18	47	20	-

45

Table 10: Charred and waterlogged plant remains from Period 3 (medieval) features (cntd)

		Sample no: 64	67	70	73†	74	76	78	79	80	81†	82	83	84	85
		Context no: 1758	1934	1799	2143	2134	2212	2235	2236	2229	2313	2486	2491	2506	2515
		Feature type: p1757	p1933	p1798	d51	d2132	occu	h2223	occu	demo	d2312	w2502	w2502	w2502	w2502
		Feature Group: PG 93	PG 96	PG 96	Enc 5	Ho 2149	B 1	B 1	B 1	B 1	P 5/6	W 2	W 2	W 2	W 2
Common name	Habitat														
Weeds etc. cntd:															
Moehringia trinervia (L.)Clairv. three-nerved sandwort	HW	-	-	-	-	4	-	-	-	-	-	-	-	-	-
Stellaria media (L.)Vill. common chickweed	CoD	-	-	-	-	31	-	-	-	-	[12]	16	3	16	3
Cerastium sp. (seed) mouse-ear	CD	-	-	-	-	25	-	-	-	-	-	-	-	1	-
Scleranthus annuus L. (achene) annual knawel	dos	-	-	-	-	-	-	-	-	-	-	-	-	-	-
Agrostemma githago L. (seed) corn cockle	A	-	-	[1]	[1]	-	-	-	-	-	[41]h	-	-	-	-
Agrostemma githago L. (fruit bracts) corn cockle	A	-	-	-	-	-	-	-	-	-	[3]	-	-	-	-
Spergula arvensis L. corn spurrey	Csa	-	-	[22]	-	-	-	-	-	-	[3]	-	-	-	1
Silene vulgaris Garcke (seed) bladder campion	GoD	-	[1]	[1]	-	-	-	-	-	-	-	-	-	-	-
Polygonum aviculare L. (achene) knotgrass	CD	-	[1]	[4]	[1]	-	-	-	-	-	[4]	11	3	19	10
Fallopia convolvulus (L.) A.Love (achene) black bindweed	AD	-	-	[3]	[3]	-	-	-	-	-	[6]	-	-	-	-
Rumex sp. (achene) dock	CDG	[9]	-	[14]	[9]	-	[1]	-	[1]	-	[99]	9	4	18	11
Rumex acetosella L. (achene) sheep's sorrel	GECas	-	[1]	[1]	[4]	-	-	-	-	-	[21]	13	12	13	8
Persicaria lapathifolia (L.)Gray (achene) pale persicaria	CDd	-	-	-	-	-	-	-	-	-	-	-	5	7	13
Persicaria maculosa Gray redshank nutlet	Cdo	-	-	-	-	6	-	-	-	-	[12]	1	5	-	29

46

The following is a dense, rotated data table of plant taxa (charred plant remains) with habitat codes and counts. Values shown in square brackets [ ] appear as bracketed counts in the original; plain numbers are unbracketed counts. A dash (–) indicates absence. Exact column alignment of the many sample columns could not be fully resolved from the rotated image; values are listed per taxon.

Taxon	Common name	Code	Recorded values
Polygonum hydropiper (L.)Spach (achene)	water pepper	Pwh	32, 5, 2, 2
Viola sp.	violet seed	GHW	1, 4; [2], [1]
Raphanus raphanistrum L. (capsule)	wild radish	CD	6, 3, 2; [4], [2], [1], [1], [1]
Thlaspi arvense L. (seed)	field penny-cress	AD	[1]
Calluna vulgaris (L.)Hull (shoot tip)	heather	EM	1, 1; [29], [2], [2], [1]
Ericaceae (fruit)	heather	–	10, 2, 2; [69], [4], [1], [1]
Primulaceae (seed)	pimpernel etc.	–	1; [1]
Rubus sect. *Glandulosa* (seed)	bramble	DHSW*	2, 14; [1]
Aphanes arvensis L. (achene)	parsley piert	Cdo	1, 14; [6], [5]
Potentilla sp. (seed)	cinquefoil	GHD	1, 1, 3, 12; [1]
Prunus domestica ssp. *Domestica* (stone)	plum	*	3
Crataegus monogyna Jacq. (stone)	hawthorn	HSW*	25; [2]
Rosa sp. (seed)	rose	HS*	1, 1; [1]
Rosaceae *Prunus/Crataegus* type (thorn)	–	–	1; [2], [1]
Rosaceae thorn *Rosa/Rubus* type	–	–	2
Trifolium/Lotus sp.	clover/trefoil	DG	[2], [1], [1]
Vicia/Lathyrus sp. (<=2mm, small seeded weed)	vetch/tare	CDG	1, 1, 2; [54], [25], [112], [6], [5], [4], [2], [1], [1]
Legume pod fragment	–	–	[2]
Aethusa cynapium L. (mericarp)	fool's parsley	CD	2, 1; [2], [1]

47

Table 10: Charred and waterlogged plant remains from Period 3 (medieval) features (cntd)

		Sample no: 64	67	70	73†	74	76	78	79	80	81†	82	83	84	85
		Context no: 1758	1934	1799	2143	2134	2212	2235	2236	2229	2313	2486	2491	2506	2515
		Feature type: p1757	p1933	p1798	d51	d2132	occu	h2223	occu	demo	d2312	w2502	w2502	w2502	w2502
		Feature Group: PG 93	PG 96	PG 96	Enc 5	Ho 2149	B 1	B 1	B 1	B 1	P 5/6	W 2	W 2	W 2	W 2
Common name	Habitat														
Weeds etc. cntd:															
Conium maculatum L. (mericarp) — hemlock	DPYw	–	–	–	–	–	–	–	–	–	–	–	–	8	1
Chaerophyllum temulum L. (mericarp) — rough chervil	GHWo	–	–	–	–	–	–	–	–	–	–	10	5	8	–
Scandix ectin-veneris L. (mericarp) — shepherd's needle	AD	–	Cf.[1]	–	–	–	–	–	–	–	–	–	–	–	–
Hyoscyamus niger L. (seed) — henbane	Dn	–	–	[1]	–	–	–	–	–	–	–	1	1	1	–
Solanum dulcamara L. (seed) — bittersweet	HYD	–	–	–	–	4	–	–	–	–	–	–	1	–	–
Lithospermum arvense L. (seed) — corn gromwell	ADG	–	–	–	[1]	–	–	–	–	–	–	–	–	–	–
Lycopus europaeus L. (nutlet) — gypsywort	FGwPB	–	–	–	–	–	–	–	–	–	–	–	–	–	–
Prunella vulgaris L. (nutlet) — selfheal	GDWo	–	–	–	–	–	–	–	–	–	–	–	–	–	3
Glechoma hederacea L. (nutlet) — ground ivy	HDWh	–	–	–	–	23	–	–	–	–	–	4	–	–	4
Lamium sp. (nutlet) — dead-nettle	CDY	–	–	–	–	9	–	–	–	–	–	–	–	–	–
cf.*Marrubium vulgare* L. (nutlet) — cf. white horehound	Gdo	–	–	–	–	–	–	–	–	–	–	–	–	–	–
Galeopsis tetrahit L. (nutlet) — common hemp-nettle	ADWod	–	–	–	–	9	–	–	–	–	[4]	8	1	10	3
Stachys sp. (nutlet) — woundwort	GHEWM	–	–	–	–	36	–	–	–	–	–	–	–	–	–

48

Taxon	Common name	Code												
Plantago lanceolata L.	ribwort plantain	Go	–	–	[2]	–	–	–	–	[1]	–	–	–	–
Odontites vernal/ Euphrasia sp.	red bartsia/ eyebright	CD	–	–	–	–	–	–	[1]	[1]	–	–	–	–
Galium aparine L.	cleavers	CDH	[1]	–	[4]	–	–	[3]	–	[1]	–	–	–	–
Anthemis cotula L. (achene)	stinking chamomile	ADhw	[7]	[157]	[34]	–	[3]	[3]	–	[393]h	3	1	5	1
Chrysanthemum segetum L. (achene)	corn marigold	AD	[2]	[2]	–	–	–	–	–	–	–	–	–	–
Tripleurospermum inodorum (L.)Sch.Bip.	scentless mayweed	CD	[1]	[41]	[5]	–	–	–	–	[6]h	–	–	–	1
Centaurea cyanus L. (achene)	cornflower	A	[1]	[19]	[1]	–	–	[1]	–	[273]h	–	–	–	1
Centaurea sp. (embryo)	cornflower	AG	–	[4]	[4]	–	–	–	–	[16]	–	–	–	–
Lapsana communis L. (achene)	nipplewort	–	–	[3]	[3]	–	–	–	–	[11]	8	1	5	2
Taraxacum sp. (achene)	dandelion	DHG	–	–	–	1	–	–	–	–	–	1	–	–
Cirsium/Carduus sp. (achene)	thistle	DHG	–	–	–	25	–	–	–	–	2	3	3	12
Sambucus nigra L. (seed)	elder	HSW*	–	–	[1]	2	–	–	–	[2]	4	–	9	6
Valerianella dentata (L.)Pollich. (fruit)	narrow-fruited corn-salad	AD	–	–	[1]	–	–	–	–	–	–	–	–	–
Lemna sp. (seed)	duckweed	MPw	–	–	–	–	–	–	–	–	–	–	5	–
Eleocharis subg. *Palustres* (nutlet)	spike-rush	MPw	–	[1]	[1]	–	–	–	–	–	–	1	–	–
Carex sp. (nutlet)	trigonous sedge	MPw	[1]	[61]	–	–	[1]	[1]	[1]	[4]	3	3	32	2
Carex sp. (nutlet)	lenticular sedge	MPw	–	–	–	5	–	–	–	–	12	–	1	36
Glyceria sp. (caryopsis)	flote-grass	PMw	–	–	–	1	–	–	–	–	–	30	6	224
Bromus sect. *Bromus* (caryopsis)	chess	ADG	–	[6]	[15]	–	–	[1]	[1]	[39]	–	–	–	–
Poaceae various (caryopsis)	small seeded grass	CDG	–	[11]	[6]	–	–	[1]	[1]	[6]	–	–	–	–

Table 10: Charred and waterlogged plant remains from Period 3 (medieval) features (cntd)

		64	67	70	73†	74	76	78	79	80	81†	82	83	84	85
Sample no:		64	67	70	73†	74	76	78	79	80	81†	82	83	84	85
Context no:		1758	1934	1799	2143	2134	2212	2235	2236	2229	2313	2486	2491	2506	2515
Feature type:		p1757	p1933	p1798	d51	d2132	occu	h2223	occu	demo	d2312	w2502	w2502	w2502	w2502
Feature Group:		PG 93	PG 96	PG 96	Enc 5	Ho 2149	B 1	B 1	B 1	B 1	P 5/6	W 2	W 2	W 2	W 2
Common name	**Habitat**														
Weeds etc. cntd:															
Poaceae *Lolium*-type (caryopsis)	*Lolium*-type grass	CDG	-	-	-	[5]	-	-	-	-	-	[1]	-	-	-	-
NFI rhizome frags	-	-	-	-	[11]	-	-	[2]	-	-	-	-	-	-	-	-
Pteridium aquilinum L. (frond frag.)	bracken	-	-	-	-	-	-	-	-	-	-	[3]	-	-	10	-
Total:		[53]	[53]	[1901]	[3560]	378	[13]	[28]	[88]	[24]	[8533]	[5] 273	[5] 112	[5] 297	[5] 460
Sample size:		40	30	40	40	10	10	20	40	10	40	10	10	10	10
Fragments/litre:		[1.3]	[1.8]	[48]	[89]	[37.8]	[1.3]	[1.4]	[2.2]	[2.4]	[213]	[0.5] 27.3	[0.5] 11.2	[0.5] 29.7	[0.5] 46.0

Table 11: Proportions of the four main medieval cereals from the three most productive samples

% of identifiable grain	wheat	barley	oats	rye	Grain:chaff:weed ratio	Frags per litre	Total no. remains
Sample <70> (pit 1798, Pit Group 96)	37%	10%	34%	19%	48:1:13	48	1901
Sample <73> (Ditch 51, Enclosure 5)	76%	14%	7%	3%	54:1:4	89	3560
Sample <81> (ditch 2312, Paddocks 5/6)	60%	5%	6%	24%	64:1:9	213	8533

weed vetches were frequent, particularly in sample <73>, which also had the highest percentage of free-threshing wheat (<2mm vetch/tare seeds = *c*. 55% of total weed seeds as opposed to 5 or 6% in the other two samples). Free-threshing wheat prefers heavier clay soils, rich in nutrients when under cultivation and requiring regular manuring to retain their fertility. Nitrogen-loving weeds such as the Chenopodiaceae were absent from the charred plant record, although they were growing around Waterhole 2 (see below). Only one taxon of weeds characteristic of acidic soils was represented in sample <73> (sheep's sorrel (*Rumex acetosella*, representing 2% of weeds), as opposed to three taxa in samples <70> and <81> (corn spurrey (*Spergula arvensis*), sheep's sorrel and wild radish (*Raphanus raphanistrum*), together representing approximately 7% and 3% of weeds respectively). Wet/damp ground weeds from sample <73> were the lowest of the three samples (17% of weeds, compared with 56% from sample <70> and 39% from sample <81>).

Leguminous crops including peas (*Pisum sativum*), Celtic beans (*Vicia faba* var. *minor*) and cultivated vetch (*Vicia sativa* ssp. *sativa*) were grown, and their occurrence with the large cereal deposits may suggest this was in rotation with cereals. Sample <70> produced the highest proportion of oats (34%), the principal weed taxa here being damp, heavy ground weeds such as stinking chamomile (*Anthemis cotula*, 40% of weeds) and sedges (*Carex* sp. = 15%). Acid ground weeds were also more frequent (7%) in this sample. The oat crop appears to have been sown in spring rather than autumn. The wheat, rye and possibly the barley were probably autumn sown, to spread the work more evenly through the year. Rye was most frequent in sample <81> (24%) but was also relatively common in sample <70> (19%). Its frequency in these two samples could be due to the cultivation of a wheat/rye maslin, as in both samples the ratio is roughly 2:1.

Of the 14 samples fully analysed, six of the samples, pits 1757 and 1933 (Pit Groups 93 and 96 respectively), occupation layers 2212 and 2236, hearth 2223 and demolition layer 2229 (all from Building 1) produced low concentrations (1.3 to 2.4 fragments per litre) of charred plant remains which primarily consisted of cereal grains. Of the identifiable grains 60% were free-threshing wheat, and a few peas (*Pisum sativum*) and a Celtic bean (*Vicia faba* var. *minor*) were present in the pits. No chaff was recovered from these samples and the range of weed taxa recorded was very similar to the rich samples. These charred deposits represent background burnt domestic waste, such as may have been swept from hearths and floors.

Four samples from successive fills of Waterhole 2 were examined, providing some indication of the type of habitat that surrounded the waterhole. Apart from the presence of a few charred cereal grains (described above), there was very little evidence for the dumping of domestic waste in the feature. This could suggest that by the time the feature became filled in, very little human activity was occurring in the area. The number of aquatic plants and marginals was fairly limited.

The plant remains from sample 74 (hollow 2149) differed markedly from those in the waterhole. The hollow was associated with Waterhole 3 (unexcavated) and lay less than a hundred metres from Waterhole 2. It seems unlikely that both features were in use at the same time. The sample may represent a later period of abandonment or reduced use of the area, as no charred plant remains were present, suggesting that manuring had ceased. The waterlogged plant assemblage contained several woodland, scrub or hedgerow species. This assemblage could be interpreted in one of two ways: either that the hollow lay within grazed pasture, with a hedge or scrub along one side or, alternately, scrub had begun to colonise the area by the time the hollow was becoming silted up, with some areas of more open grassland remaining. This hollow remained undated and was only exposed at the base of a section through a post-medieval field boundary running north-west to south-east through the site.

Insect remains, by David Smith

Three samples (<82>, <83> and <84>) of waterlogged material were selected for insect analysis, from medieval Waterhole 2. The aim was to ascertain the local environmental conditions and the use of the waterhole.

The samples were paraffin floated using the standard method of Kenward *et al.* (1980). Each sub-sample weighed 8.5kg and totalled 10 litres in volume. Identification was by direct comparison to the Goraham and Girling collections of British Coleoptera. The taxonomy follows that of Lucht (1987). Each species has been assigned to one or more ecological groupings. These follow a simplified version of Robinson (1981; 1983). The occurrence of each of the ecological groupings is expressed as a percentage in Fig. 19. The

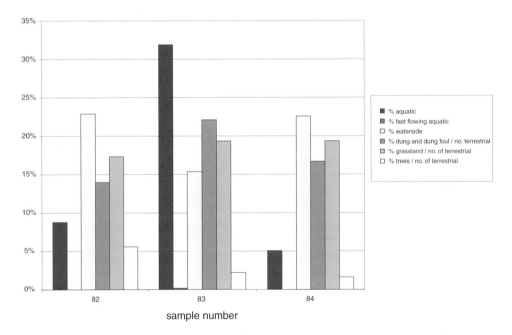

Fig. 19: Proportions of ecological groupings for Coleoptera

pasture/grassland, dung and woodland/timber beetle species are calculated as percentages of the number of terrestrial species, as opposed to the whole fauna.

Discussion

The insect faunas are characteristic of an open, farmed and grazed landscape. This is indicated by the species of 'ground beetle' recovered. *Nebria brevicollis, Loricera pilicornis, Clivina fossor*, many of the *Bembidion* and *Trechus* species, *Harpalus rufipes, H. aenea, Pterostichus melanarius, P. madidus, Calathus fuscipes* and *Amara aulica* are all associated with open ground, meadows, cultivated fields and wasteland (Lindroth 1974). Several of the ground beetles recovered are associated with open, dry and sandy ground. Examples are *Carabus avensis, Notiophilus hypocrita, Bradycellus harpalinus* and *Dromius linearis*. Similar conditions are suggested by the phytophages (plant feeders) since their hosts are often typical of open ground, cultivated land and waste areas. For example, *Brachypterus urticae, Apion urticarium* and *Cidnorhinus quadrimaculatus* indicate the presence of stands of stinging nettle (*Urtica dioica* L.) possibly around the edges of Waterhole 2. Local patches of clover (*Trifolium* spp.), vetches (*Vicia* spp.) and medicks (*Medicago* spp.) are indicated by the various species of *Apion* and *Sitona. Alophus triguttatus* and *Gymentron* spp. indicate plantains (*Plantago* spp.) and *Gastrodea viridula, Apion marchicum* and *Phytobius* are associated with the presence of docks (*Rumex* spp.). Many other species, such as elaterid 'click beetles' and cantharid 'soldier beetles' are often associated with open areas and grassland. In total Coleoptera typical of grass/meadow habitats account for 17–20% of the terrestrial fauna recovered, suggesting that grassland and waste ground are a dominant part of the local landscape.

Pasture may also have been an important component of the landscape surrounding Waterhole 2. The *Geotrupes* and *Aphodius* 'dung beetles', which are associated with the dung of grazing herbivores, account for 14–22% of the terrestrial fauna. These species have a wide flight potential and, as a result, it is difficult to suggest how near pasture may have been. *Onthophilus striatus*, the *Oxytelus* spp., *Platystethus arenarius* and several of the *Ceryon* species are also often associated with cow and sheep dung.

There is almost no evidence for woodland, thus the area may have been extensively cleared. The only species recovered that is directly indicative of a specific tree is the 'bark beetle' *Hylesinus crenatus*, which lives on ash (*Fraxinus* spp.). This is confirmed by the presence of ash in the charcoal assemblage (see *Charcoal*, above). The *Polydrusus* and *Rhynchaenus* species are associated with the foliage of trees but this can be isolated scrub and trees rather than dense woodland. The interpretation of the charcoal assemblage is that woodland was located away from the site (Lindroth 1974).

It is likely that these insects were deposited into an open and clear body of water. The water beetles recovered, such as *Hydroporus rufifrons* and the various *Hydreana* and *Octhebius*, are typical of bodies of slow flowing or still water (Hansen 1987; Nilsson and Holmen 1995). *Hydrochus elongatus* is thought to be particularly associated with stagnant water (Hansen 1987). There appears to have been little surface or waterside vegetation in the pool, with the exception of some duckweed (*Lemna* spp.) indicated by the presence of the small weevil *Tanysphyrus lemnae*.

The insect remains are consistent with the interpretation of this feature as a waterhole. There is no evidence from the insects recovered that settlement material has contributed to these deposits. The best comparisons are probably the Romano-British period waterholes at Daventry Rail Freight Terminal, Northamptonshire (Smith 1999), and at Whitemoor Haye, Staffordshire (Smith 2002), where similar insect faunas were recovered.

DISCUSSION

By Mary Alexander, Timothy Darvill and Jonathan Hart

Six main phases of activity are represented in the archaeological evidence from Blenheim Farm, each providing valuable insights on settlement and society in the upper Evenlode Valley from the Pleistocene through to the Middle Ages. The following sections summarise what was found in each phase, and situate the evidence within its wider archaeological and social context.

Palaeolithic (Period 0), by Timothy Darvill

The flint cordiform handaxe made on a cobble of yellow-brown flint recovered as an unstratified find emphasises the potential of the Cotswold uplands as a source of artefacts from the late glacial occupation of the Midland Plain. Sumbler (2001) has shown that the Moreton Drift, also known as the Wolston Formation, can be sub-divided into several elements, including two separate deposits of glacial outwash gravel. The first, the Moreton Member, is characterised by Trias-derived erratic material originating to the north-west. It relates to Oxygen Isotope Stage 12 (OIS 12) within the Anglian Glacial Stage and therefore dates to before 400,000 BP. It is these deposits that choked the headwaters of the pre-Anglian Bytham River system, thereby creating suitable conditions for the subsequent formation of the Avon, Stour and Thames drainage system (Lang and Keen 2005, 75). The second, the Oadby Member, is characterised by younger flint-dominated erratics and dates to OIS 10, a cold phase during the early Wolstonian dating to about 350,000 BP. It is unlikely that the flint handaxe is residual within, or contemporary with, either of these drift deposits since it is not heavily rolled and is typologically too late for an early Wolstonian (or earlier) origin. It may, however, have been made locally from a cobble derived from Oadby Member deposits. Most plausible is a connection with hunter-gatherer groups camping near the shores of Lake Harrison, a proglacial lake immediately south of the late Wolstonian ice sheets on the Midland Plain during OIS 6, *c.* 120,000 BP (Douglas 1980, 281; Roe 1981, 49). Covering the area from Moreton-in-Marsh in the south to Leicester in the north, and from Rugby in the east to Birmingham in the west, this lake would have survived into the warm phases of the early Ipswichian (OIS 5), and been very attractive to migrating animal herds; hippopotamus is amongst the species recorded in a rich OIS 5 fauna from nearby Eckington, Worcestershire (Keen and Bridgland 1986). Although Ashton and Lewis (2002) argue that there is little certain evidence for human populations in Britain between the end of OIS 7 and some unspecified time during OIS 4, they accept that 'sooner or later rich archaeological sites of this age will be found' in the West Midlands (2002, 79). While the Blenheim Farm handaxe is strictly undated its form would be consistent with a Mousterian context so its presence at Moreton may point the way towards more Middle Palaeolithic discoveries in the area sooner rather than later.

The presence of a light scatter of struck flints and occasional worked pieces from the 7th through to the 3rd millennium BC is entirely consistent with early post-glacial occupation of the area by hunter-gatherer, hunter-gardener and early farming communities. However, the absence of evidence for much use of the area during the 4th and 3rd millennia is curious given the relatively intensive occupation of the Cotswolds through this period (Darvill 1987, 33–65; 2006, 18–35). It suggests that the upper Evenlode Valley remained wooded well into the early 2nd millennium BC.

16th–14th centuries BC (Period 1: early), by Timothy Darvill

The first substantial phase of occupation at Blenheim Farm comprises four roundhouses, pit clusters, a waterhole, tree-throw pits, and a boundary ditch seemingly marking the north and west sides of an occupation area naturally delimited to the south and east sides by a small stream (Fig. 1). The full extent of the features associated with this phase may be partly truncated by later activity, especially the Roman and medieval enclosures, compounds and field systems, but the surviving evidence provides a fair picture of activity for a period that until now was more or less invisible in the north Cotswolds. Four radiocarbon determinations on short-lived specimens from CPBS1 and CPBS3, and Pit 1860 in Pit Group 12, span the period *c.* 1600 BC through to *c.* 1300 BC, centred on the mid 14th century BC. This falls within Period 5 of Needham's (1996; Needham *et al.* 1997) subdivision of the British Bronze Age, conventionally the later Middle Bronze Age, during which time metalwork of Acton Park 2, Taunton, and Penard industrial phases was in circulation, and Deverel-Rimbury pottery characterises domestic assemblages. Across the British Isles it was a period of change, which Colin Burgess links to upheavals across much of Europe as a result of the collapse of the Mycenaean and Hittite empires (1980, 155–9; but cf. Needham 1996, 134). Certainly, new kinds of settlement appeared, occupation expanded into previously under-used territory, and technical innovations stimulated new kinds of metalwork. It is against such a background that the appearance of a wholly new settlement on seemingly virgin land at Blenheim Farm should be seen.

Topographically the Bronze Age settlement occupies an ideal position: a natural knoll of slightly higher ground with a southerly aspect and ready access to water. Pollen sequences from the Tewkesbury area suggest fairly extensive deforestation during the middle and late second millennium BC (Brown 1982; 1983; Brown and Barber 1985) and at Blenheim Farm isolated and clustered tree-throw pits within and to the north of the settlement area have been recorded. These suggest some partial clearance of the landscape before occupation began, with continued periodic removal of remaining trees over the following centuries, a practice that has been noted at other sites of the second and early first millennium BC in the Thames Valley (Moore and Jennings 1992, 13 and fig. 6). Two tree-throw pits contained material likely to belong with the early Period 1 occupation; many of the others are technically undated but contained similar fills and may therefore have been associated with the same sequence of clearance events. West of the circular post-built structures (CPBS), tree-throw pit 1063 contained a small assemblage of fresh flintworking debitage. Rather more unusual is tree-throw pit 1008, which contained three flint flakes and, in the lower fill, the cremated remains of an adult human. This is the only evidence for burial practices preserved on the site, although it should be borne in mind that soil conditions were not conducive to the survival of unburnt bone. Tree-throw pit 1008 is one of a small cluster of eight such pits immediately south of Waterhole 1 that may together have formed a highly visible landscape feature: a stand of mature trees atop a low but prominent knoll. It is tempting to speculate that following the loss of these ancient trees, perhaps in a gale or as the result of a natural catastrophe, one of the resulting pits was chosen for the ritual deposition of a cremation. Similar evidence has been noted at Reading Business Park, Berkshire, where a single cremation dated to 1688–1431 BC was added to a much earlier monument, perhaps to strengthen ancestral ties to the land (Brossler 2001, 133).

Ditch 1, L-shaped in plan, provides a clearly defined northern and western boundary to the settlement area, running around the contour of the hill. The ditch was up to 3m wide, a shallow V-form in cross-section, and survived to a maximum depth of 1.3m. There was no evidence of recutting, and only its slightly asymmetric middle fill suggests the former presence of an internal bank. The 2.6m-wide gap opening to the north is taken to be an entrance causeway; its unelaborated form confirms the idea that this insubstantial construction with its incomplete circuit cannot be considered a defensive feature in any meaningful sense. Rather it should be considered as a north-facing facade formally marking the entrance to a compound or occupation area whose other boundaries may well have been marked at the time with light fences, hedges, natural features in the landscapes, or simply a fall-off in the intensity of activity. Charred fragments of blackthorn and hawthorn recovered from the ditch fills may be indirect evidence of hedging alongside the ditch or in areas to the south and east where the ditch is absent. A collection of flint nodules on the floor of the ditch and fresh flint debitage in the lower fills suggests that tool-making may have been carried out near the margins of the settlement but there is no indication that the boundary ditch was systematically used for the disposal of domestic debris and waste. A pollen sequence through the ditch fills suggests construction in a fairly dry environment followed by fairly rapid natural filling. The area defined by the ditch is a minimum of 100m east–west and 80m north–south, but it is unclear whether the full extent of the ditch, which extended beyond the excavated area, originally defined two or three sides of an 'enclosure'. Comparable examples of both can be cited from the second half of the 2nd millennium BC in southern Britain and are generally known as 'Martin Down Style Enclosures' after a type-site excavated by Pitt Rivers in Dorset (Piggott 1942; Barrett *et al.* 1983; Edmonds 1989). At Angle Ditch, Dorset, just two sides of an area with minimum dimensions of 50m by 25m are defined by a ditch up to 2m deep and with no sign of an accompanying bank (Barrett *et al.* 1991, 219–22). Boscombe Down East, Wiltshire, has three sides marked by ditches, although the western side is incomplete; the main entrance opens to the north (Stone 1936). The more recently excavated example at Down Farm, Dorset, has two-and-a-half sides, encloses a minimum area 35m by 25m, and had a bank immediately inside the ditch. During phase 2 at this site, dated by a series of radiocarbon determinations to *c.* 1495–1310 BC, the internal settlement was bounded by a light fence and comprised a roundhouse *c.* 9m in diameter, two ancillary structures each *c.* 6.5m across, a small pond and a yard (Barrett *et al.* 1991, 183–211). Larger examples include Martin Down, Dorset, which is *c.* 100m by 60m (Barrett *et al.* 1991, 220) and Ogbourne Down West, Wiltshire, with a more sinuous outline, *c.* 115m by 60m, and perhaps of more than one phase (Piggott 1942, 52). Within the overall range of such sites, Blenheim Farm is therefore towards the larger end of the spectrum (Fig. 20) and also the most northerly example currently known.

The partial character of the settlement boundary at Blenheim Farm and elsewhere may seem rather odd to modern eyes, but as already indicated this may in part be the result of an incomplete archaeological record. A stream flowing close to the eastern and southern edges of the site at the time of the excavation may reflect the route of an ancient watercourse delimiting Period 1 occupation in these directions. Certainly, where the stream runs close to the southern edge of the site it seems to describe an arc that forms a mirror image of the boundary ditch to the north (Figs 1 and 21). It is possible, therefore, that the boundary ditch was keyed into an existing landscape feature, and that the 'enclosure' was formed by a ditch along its northern and western sides and by a stream along its southern and eastern sides.

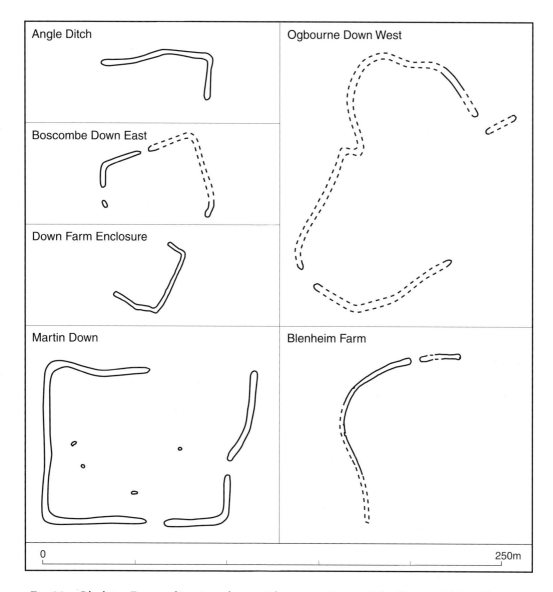

Fig. 20:   Blenheim Farm prehistoric enclosure with comparative sites (after Piggott 1942 and Barrett et al. 1991; scale 1:2000)

Contemporary with the enclosure boundary were four CPBSs, ranging from 5m to 7m in diameter. In each the walls were defined by a single ring of postholes although other postholes both inside and outside the wall-line are considered to be part of the overall structure. The entrances probably opened to the south-east although there is little evidence for porches or elaborated portals. CPBS4 probably had a central support. CPBS1 and 3 must have been successive and, while it is noticeable that both appear to have had spreads of material immediately outside the doorways, it is impossible to say

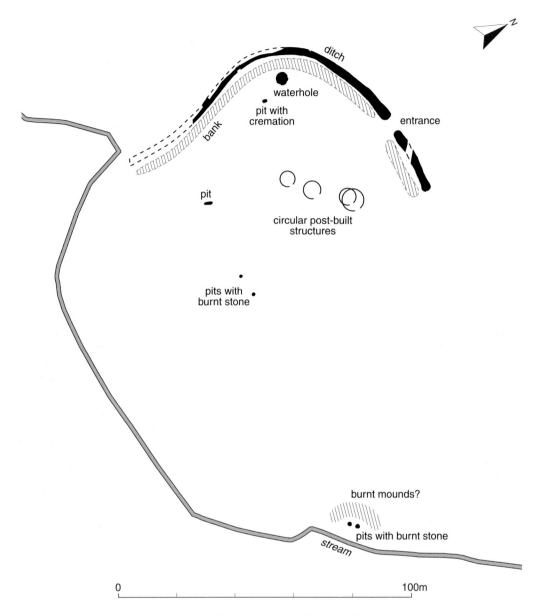

Fig. 21: Diagrammatic representation of the prehistoric enclosure (scale 1:1250)

which of the two structures was earlier. Theoretically, a maximum of three out of the four recorded structures could have stood at any one time, but given the evidence for replacement represented by CPBS1 and 3 it seems pragmatic to think in terms of two structures at a time with two main phases of construction. Since none of the floors in these structures survived, little can be said about the purpose or the social use of space within each, although it may be suggested that at any one time there was a main dwelling together with an ancillary building such as a storehouse or workshop. CPBS1 is dated to 1430–1300 BC on the basis of two radiocarbon determinations on wheat grain from posthole 1101 (3109±31 BP: Wk-17813 and 3063±31 BP: Wk-17814), and was associated with Deverel-Rimbury Ware. CPBS3 dates to 1430–1260 BC on the basis of a single radiocarbon determination on hazel charcoal (3080±31 BP: Wk-17812) and was likewise associated with Deverel-Rimbury style pottery.

Two main architectural styles have been recognised amongst the round timber structures of the late second millennium BC in Britain: single post-ring buildings, and double post-ring buildings (Nowakowski 1991, 184–88). The Blenheim Farm CPBSs are entirely typical of the first style, and examples have been found right across southern Britain. Those at Down Farm, Dorset, have already been mentioned as they lie within a Martin Down Style Enclosure. They are exactly contemporary with those at Blenheim Farm according to available radiocarbon dates and show many affinities in size and design, although the main dwelling in Phase 2 at Down Farm seems to have had a well-defined porch while the ancillary buildings did not (Barrett *et al*. 1991, 186–95). Other contemporary sites with comparable architecture include, from west to east, Trethellan Farm, Newquay, Cornwall (Nowakowski 1991), Shearplace Hill, Dorset (Rahtz and ApSimon 1962), and Black Patch, East Sussex (Drewett 1979). Nothing of quite the same date is yet known in the Cotswold region, but from around the turn of the first millennium BC are the twenty or more CPBSs at Shorncote, Gloucestershire. Three main groups can be recognized, none of them enclosed, each representing a discrete occupation area (Darvill 2006, 40–1, with earlier refs.). The structures range in size from 4.5m up to 10m in diameter, and most are of single post-ring design. The majority had porches flanking doors opening to the south-east, and a few had internal posts.

A waterhole situated near the core of the Blenheim Farm settlement was excavated. It is undated, but its fills and form suggest a close association with the Period 1 occupation. Similar waterholes are known from many settlements of the later 2nd and early 1st millennium BC, including Kemerton, Worcestershire (Jackson and Napthan 1998, 62), Shorncote (Hearne and Heaton 1994, 21–31, 48–9), and Reading Business Park, Berkshire (Brossler 2001, 133–4). Occasionally, such features had a secondary use as rubbish disposal pits (Jackson and Napthan 1998, 62) but while the tip lines exhibited by the main fills of Waterhole 1 were suggestive of backfilling, the material seems to have been clean topsoil with almost no anthropogenic inclusions other than a few burnt stones.

More than a dozen pits, also undated and variously of round or crescent-shaped outline, may also be associated with the settlement on the basis of their horizontal stratigraphy. To the south-east, Pit Group 12 was distinctive in containing abundant burnt stones. A radiocarbon determination on charcoal from pit 1860 of 1610–1420 BC (3225±32 BP: Wk-17816) is accepted as dating the feature; a second determination falling in the 11th century AD is considered intrusive. Pit Group 134 also contained burnt stones and while undated may be related. All the pits in the vicinity of the stream (Group 12) contain burnt stones and may be remnants of one or more burnt mounds of the type increasingly recognised beside streams in the south Midlands (Barfield and Hodder 1987); examples have been excavated at Frocester (Darvill 2000) and Leckhampton (Leah and Young 2001) in the Cotswolds. Whether such features were cooking places, industrial work-areas involving hot-rock technology, or had some kind of ceremonial role as feasting places or sweat-lodges remains to be determined. Pit Group 10 outside the enclosure to the north comprised small holes that could have been postholes, but were most likely shallow pits just possibly for ceremonial purposes.

Overall, the mid 2nd millennium BC settlement at Blenheim Farm should be seen as a small farmstead, perhaps occupied by a single extended family whose dwelling, ancillary buildings, water supply, working spaces and yards were sheltered within the embrace of a Martin Down Style Enclosure with its most grandiose aspect facing north. Their material culture was seemingly relatively poor, but they certainly made and used flint tools, and may well have had metal objects too. Their pottery was manufactured locally in the Deverel-Rimbury style suggesting cultural links to the south and south-east; the assemblage, although small, is the first in the area to be securely dated.

Evidence for the nature of the environment around the site remains difficult to interpret. The absence of damp-loving ground weeds in the environmental sequences examined indicates generally dry conditions. The low-level presence of charcoal from wetland tree species may reflect a genuine absence of such species from the environs of the site, but it is possible that their use for building material rather than for fuel has resulted in under-representation amongst the charred plant remains. If it is assumed that Waterhole 1, whose depth was not much greater than that of the ditch, functioned successfully it seems probable that the southern part of the ditch, and the stream bed into which it extended, contained standing water when first cut.

There is very little evidence for cereal processing at the site, a similarity it shares with the slightly later settlements at Kemerton, Worcestershire (Jackson and Napthan 1998), and Shorncote (Darvill 2006, 40). It may also be noted that storage pits and above-ground granaries are absent at Blenheim Farm. This contrasts with general propositions of widespread arable intensification in the later 2nd millennium BC across southern England (e.g. Campbell and Straker 2003), and claims based on higher concentrations of charred cereal processing waste found on larger settlement sites dating to the period after 1200 BC (Jones 1981). Clearly there were regional differences in the subsistence practices followed, with some areas more dependent on cultivation and others focused on animal husbandry. Unfortunately, direct evidence for the nature and quantity of livestock maintained by the Blenheim Farm community is missing because of the poor preservation of bone in the generally acidic soils in the area. The only faunal remains from Period 1, the sheep/goat mandible, came from an animal whose age at death suggests that it was kept for wool production or for breeding.

The importance of the Blenheim Farm site lies in the broad landscape context provided by the investigation of the surrounding area. Unlike the later 2nd millennium BC settlements in the middle Thames region, for example at Reading Business Park, Berkshire (Brossler 2001), and Heathrow T5, Middlesex (FA 2006), the occupation area is not integrated within a contemporary field system. Rather, it must be seen as a semi-open site, lying beside a small watercourse within a comparatively open landscape perhaps with small garden-sized cultivation plots and extensive grazing lands and wood-pasture beyond. However, patterning to the social use of space, in which the dwellings and ancillary structures form the focus of the settlement on the higher and drier ground, pits lie round about, occasional ceremonial deposits and structures lie fully integrated with the domestic space, and burnt mounds for special events, industry and cooking lie adjacent to the nearest watercourse, is entirely typical, whether or not associated with a Martin Down Style Enclosure (Fig. 21). At South Lodge Camp, Dorset, for example, two CPBSs, one larger than the other and probably representing a house and an ancillary building, stood immediately south-east of a burnt mound, the whole arrangement being set within an enclosure (Barrett *et al.* 1991, 209). Much the same can be observed at Shearplace Hill, Dorset, where there is a pond rather than a burnt mound (Rahtz and ApSimon 1962), and at Black Patch, East Sussex, where an unenclosed settlement comprised five structures and two ponds (Drewett 1979, fig. 1). At Heathrow T5, Middlesex, waterholes and burnt mounds were found associated with occupation debris and structures of the later 2nd millennium BC, but the buildings are unlike others of the period noted above (FA 2006, 114–47). Further upstream in the middle Thames Valley investigations at Reading Business Park in 1986–8 and 1995 revealed a long-lived occupation site of the later 2nd and early 1st millennium BC, with perhaps as many as twenty round buildings in clusters anything from 10m to 50m to the south-west of an equally long-lived burnt mound that flanked a palaeochannel. Waterholes and pits were also present, the whole arrangement being set within the framework of a rectilinear field system that was probably established early in the 2nd millennium BC (Brossler 2001, with earlier refs). Fragmentary traces of what must be the same overall pattern but with no evidence of contemporary field systems have been excavated in the upper Thames Valley at Roughground Farm (Allen *et al.* 1993). Here occupation dated to between 1500 and 1000 BC comprised a scatter of nine pits and a human inhumation. Traces of any structures present would probably have been lost through agriculture or the methods of topsoil stripping used. Crucially, no evidence of arable cultivation was found, and amongst the animal bones recovered sheep outnumbered cattle by nearly four to one (Allen *et al.* 1993, 34–5) suggesting that even off the limestone uplands proper a pastoral economy prevailed.

Evidence of other settlements of the later 2nd millennium BC on the Cotswolds and adjoining areas of the upper Thames Valley and Severn Valley is scant, although gradually building as a result of development-related projects taking investigations into new areas. Traces of what may tentatively be regarded as small farmsteads have been noted at a handful of sites (Darvill 2006, 42) but none are yet fully published. The same applies to what may turn out to be a direct comparison for Blenheim Farm: an L-shaped enclosure containing roundhouses, pits and a fence-line investigated at the Cotswold Community site, Somerford Keynes, in 2003 (Weaver 2004). At Frocester in the Severn Valley excavations have revealed a linear boundary, burnt mound, and scattered traces of occupation (Price 2000), while further north at Hucclecote there are burials dating to the 14th–12th centuries BC but as yet no direct evidence of structures and occupation (Thomas *et al.* 2003, 8–9). Further north still, near the confluence of the Severn and Avon at Tewkesbury, there is clear evidence of occupation on the valley floor. A small 'D'-shaped enclosure and a curvilinear ditch were found on the east side of a slight promontory between the Tirle Brook and River Swilgate. Investigations in 1991–7 showed that these features date to the later 2nd millennium BC and connect with a series of linear boundaries seen also in nearby excavations that may have been linked with animal husbandry and small-scale cultivation within a fairly structured valley-floor landscape (Walker *et al.* 2004, 85–7). Quite different in character is the hilltop enclosure at Stow on the Wold, which appears to have been constructed in the period around 1390–970 BC, perhaps as one of a series of regional exchange centres scattered across southern Britain (Darvill 2006, 42).

The tradition of building round barrows, of which there are several hundred scattered across the Gloucestershire Cotswolds and adjacent areas, as burial places was largely over by 1500 BC, and the later 2nd millennium BC is characterised by cremation burials either singly or in cemeteries. The isolated cremation in tree-throw pit 1008 is wholly within the expected range of deposits and its presence within an occupation area is not unusual. Elsewhere in the north Cotswolds single cremations within urns have been found at Cow Common and Lower Swell (Darvill 1987, 108–9) while about 9km to the east of Blenheim Farm excavations around the Kingstone at Rollright, Oxfordshire, revealed a small cremation cemetery overlying earlier round barrows and here seemingly marked by a standing stone (Lambrick 1988, 70–80). The largest such cemetery so far known in the area lies about 11km to the west of Blenheim Farm at Bevan's Quarry (O'Neil 1967). Here excavation of a round barrow (Temple Guiting 8) revealed a cemetery of at least five cremation deposits representing six or more men women and children cut into the top of the barrow mound. It is likely that the cemetery extended beyond the excavated area, perhaps as far as the adjacent Temple Guiting 3 barrow where fragments of broken urns have been found (Darvill 1987, 108). The Deverel-Rimbury style urns at Bevan's Quarry are very similar to those from Blenheim Farm in terms of form and fabric, although the site is probably too distant to have been directly connected. Richard Bradley (1981, 100) has shown that in central southern Britain cemeteries were typically situated less than 700m from their associated settlement, often with the cemetery northwards of the settlement. In the case of Blenheim Farm attention might usefully be directed to the area east of Dorn Roman settlement (Fig. 1), in a search for contemporary burials.

Landscapes of the later 2nd millennium BC in western Britain often contain natural places that had special meaning to the lives of local communities and which were often used for the deposition of metalwork as gifts to local deities and spirits of the earth (Bradley 1990). Spring, rivers and bogs seem to have been particularly favoured and in this connection the discovery in 1952 of a basal-looped bronze spearhead near a spring in Batsford Park (Neville Terry 1953) may be especially relevant as this piece belongs to the Taunton or Acton Park industrial traditions and would therefore have been contemporary with the occupation at Blenheim Farm just 2.5km away to the east.

8th–5th centuries BC (Period 1: late), by Timothy Darvill

Evidence for activity at Blenheim Farm during Late Bronze Age and Early Iron Age, broadly speaking the 8th through to 5th centuries BC, is restricted to some or all of the pits within Pit Group 9 and the tree-throw pit 1248 some c. 90m to the north-west. All are united in being associated with bipartite bowl and bowl/jar forms of pottery of post-Deverel-Rimbury tradition made in a series of sandy fabrics. The pits are generally small, between 0.4m and 0.8m across and up to 0.2m deep. They are clearly not storage pits, and some kind of ceremonial use involving the deposition of offering may be suspected (a large number of hazelnut shells were present in pit 1331). Their position north of Pit Group 10 may also be relevant (see above). Tree-throw pit 1248 contained oak charcoal, possibly from the tree that formerly grew there and may have been a long-lived and well-known landscape feature.

Romano-British (2nd century AD), by Jonathan Hart

The Romano-British features had been truncated by ploughing and shallower features may have been entirely lost. However, the recovered plan suggests that the field system was broadly contemporary with Enclosures 1 and 2, with Enclosure 3 being later. The key question relating to the enclosures is whether they enclosed buildings, and thus mark settlement, or whether they had a purely agricultural function. No evidence for structures was recovered, although it is possible that the often ephemeral traces of buildings may not have survived. Small ditched enclosures of similar form to those found here have been viewed as marking the locations of buildings at some sites in the Thames valley such as Totterdown Lane (Pine and Preston 2004) and Old Shifford Farm (Hey 1995), frequently in the absence of surviving structural evidence. The most compelling evidence against the interpretation of Romano-British features at Blenheim Farm as a farmstead, however, is the very low quantities of artefacts recovered. The few sherds recovered were small and abraded, suggesting secondary deposition following manuring rather than a primary deposition as domestic waste within the ditches.

On balance, the enclosures at Blenheim Farm are best interpreted as stock pens, perhaps with internal upcast banks surmounted by hedges or fencing. Small amounts of blackthorn and hawthorn charcoal, typical hedge species, were recovered from Enclosure 2 but do not have a secure provenance. The enclosures can be compared with 1st to 2nd-century AD Roman examples at Thornhill Farm in the Upper Thames valley, where units of two or three conjoined enclosures, of slightly smaller dimensions than those at Blenheim Farm, were interpreted as stock-rearing pens (Jennings et al. 2004, 150), despite similarly narrow entrances.

Medieval (c. 11th–14th centuries AD), by Mary Alexander

Material evidence for activity spanning the period between the Roman field system and the earliest medieval field boundaries is not present in the archaeological record, although the plan of the latter hints at either continuity or a survival of some Roman boundary alignments as landscape features. Reforestation of the Cotswolds region was sufficiently widespread by the 7th century for the Saxon name to reflect its wooded aspect ('wolds' meaning woodland; Dyer 2002). However, at Blenheim Farm it is apparent that when the medieval field boundaries were established, some remnants of the Roman field system were still present, as the boundary of the Roman Enclosure 1, the southern side of Enclosure 3 and ditch 2105 were incorporated into the later field system.

The origin of the settlement that preceded the planned town of the 13th century at Moreton-in-Marsh is not known, although an early 8th-century presence is suggested in a charter of AD 714 and the place-name 'Moretune' is referred to in the Domesday survey of 1086 (Moore 1982, 19.2). The genesis of the village would appear typical of the region, in that the excavated evidence suggests settlement in its present location dates to the 11th century (Dyer 2002; Langton et al. 2000). At this time the scattered farms and hamlets that were a feature of the rural landscape began to be abandoned in favour of nucleated settlements, many of which continue as village locations up to the present day. The land surrounding these nascent villages was worked as extensive open fields, most typically two fields in which each villager worked individual strips of land, and in which a two-course rotation between arable and pasture was undertaken. Moreton-in-Marsh had two documented open fields; the land at Blenheim Farm lay to the north of 'Lower Field', which was to the east of the settled area. The evidence of cultivation at Tinker's Close displays a radical realignment of the ridge-and-furrow on two occasions between the 11th and 13th centuries, possibly reflecting more than one reorganisation of the land in this transitional period (Langton *et al.* 2000). Blenheim Farm occupies an area on the boundary of the parishes of Moreton and Batsford, and there is no evidence for ridge-and-furrow cultivation, although the shallow Roman features on the western side of the site suggest truncation by later agricultural practices.

The medieval activity at Blenheim Farm was predominantly rural and falls into two main phases. The earlier phase (A) featuring ditches delineating small enclosures is superseded by much larger fields (Phase B). The small pens or paddocks of the earlier phase with their streamside location may have been for sheep, as opposed to cattle, which would not have been kept in big herds at this time (C. Dyer, pers. comm.). Similar small land divisions are cited in manorial records in association with other elements of medieval sheep management. Separate pens or paddocks enable the carrying out of a wide manner of tasks including counting and, if necessary, dividing sheep belonging to different owners, or separating pregnant animals for lambing. A system of small enclosures also facilitates sheep shearing and allows sick or diseased animals to be divided from the flock (Dyer 1995, 149–50). The stream would have been a convenient supply of drinking water for the livestock and for those tending the flocks as well as for washing sheep and fleeces. Cattle and sheep/goat are present in the bone assemblage in roughly equal quantities, with smaller quantities of pig, horse and dog also present. The faunal remains are more likely to reflect the general diet of the farmer/shepherd and local supply of material used to manure the fields, rather than the livestock kept in the enclosures at the site.

Small pens and enclosures have been recorded by excavation and earthwork surveys in several locations in the north Cotswolds, although with considerable variety of layout and dimensions; some, like the examples at Blenheim Farm, incorporate surviving elements of Romano-British field systems (Dyer 1995, 146–7). All examples noted from earthwork survey display raised enclosure boundaries, denoting banks or walls, while at Blenheim Farm there is no evidence to suggest this, although there may have been delineation by fences or hedges. Within a few kilometres of Blenheim Farm, at Chalk Hill, Temple Guiting, nine enclosures were recorded of similar dimensions to those at Blenheim Farm, varying from 10m to 30m in length (Dyer 1995, 141). Close by, at Kineton Hill (also Temple Guiting), six larger enclosures measuring 20–40m wide and 60–80m long were surveyed (Dyer 1996, fig. 7). More similar to those at Chalk Hill and Blenheim Farm were two or three enclosures measuring 20m by 20m, surveyed at Manless Town, Brimpsfield (Dyer 1995, 146).

These enclosures, and other examples from the archaeological record, were found in association with sheepcotes, a form of rural structure that featured in large numbers in the north Cotswold landscape. These buildings would have housed the sheep at night during the winter months, and provided a sheltered place to feed the flocks hay and fodder when grazing was insufficient. Surviving examples are most numerous in marginal locations, often on the edges of the arable lowland where they would have served to manage flocks grazing on upland pasture in the summer months and at other times on stubble and fallow fields. Manure from the sheepcote would have been collected for enriching the arable soils. These structures were a feature of manorial estates and feature in the documents of estate management in the 13th–15th centuries (Dyer 1996). Manorial sheepcotes are recognised as long narrow buildings averaging 42m in length divided into stalls, accommodating flocks of up to 300 sheep. Less visible in the archaeological record, but frequently mentioned in manorial court roles, were the peasant sheepcotes. Examples recorded in court rolls indicate that a typical structure would be of two or three bays, 9–14m long, built with a cruck-framed superstructure on stone foundations. A single excavated example of a two-bay structure that could have served this purpose is from the deserted medieval settlement at Upton. This building measured 9.5m by 4.5m with evidence for a pitched stone floor (Dyer 1995, 159).

The sheepcote was often accompanied by smaller rectangular structures. It is apparent from the documentary sources, and evidence from rarely excavated examples, that the sheepcote or ancillary structures were occupied by the shepherd, dairymaid and other farm workers on an occasional or seasonal basis, including the lambing season when the sheepcote functioned as a lambing shed. An ancillary building, if made secure, could be used to store valuable medicines, equipment and possibly the fleeces that would accumulate during the year as sheep died. The lower stone courses of such a building survived at Chalk Hill, Temple Guiting, where it was located at right angles to the end of a large sheepcote. The building was rectangular, measuring approximately 9m by 4.4m, and was equipped with at least one barred window (Baldwin and O'Neil 1958, 63). Further examples of these ancillary buildings have been recorded at Elmont in Beckford, Worcestershire, where the building contained a hearth, and at Kineton, Temple Guiting. Finds from these structures and the associated sheepcotes date to the 13th–15th centuries (Dyer 1995, 147).

In the light of this evidence it seems likely that the poorly preserved Building 1 at Blenheim Farm should be interpreted either as a more humble peasant sheepcote, or an ancillary building for storage and the seasonal accommodation of shepherds. The eastern wall of Building 1 could have served as an internal division to a small sheepcote of two bays; the southern extent of the building and the absent wall indicated by the extent of the hollow, giving an approximate length of 9m to the structure and a minimum width of 2.5m. However the presence of a possible hearth and the quantity of domestic waste are more consistent with an interpretation as a dwelling, albeit one that may only have been seasonally occupied. Given the relatively low-lying position, if flocks were kept on the site during the winter months they could have been sheltered at night in a less substantial building, not apparent from the archaeological record. The remnant of a spread of stones in Paddock 4 to the west and the postholes and pits (Groups 91 and 93) to the south of this feature may indicate the alternative location of a structure of this kind.

The flocks at Blenheim Farm may have been driven to nearby fields to feed on stubble left by arable cultivation and to graze in fallow periods, returning valuable manure to the fields before the new crop was sown. The flocks could have been driven to pasture on higher and more marginal land in the summer months, but there is environmental evidence from the paddock ditches and pits to suggest crops grown for fodder, such as oats and rye, supplemented the food acquired from grazing. Of particular note in this context is the high percentage of burnt oat and rye grain found close to Building 1 in pit 1798, although in general the environmental evidence is typical of human domestic waste, reflecting the diet available to the occupants of the building (see *Charred and waterlogged plant remains*, above).

The impetus for the reorganisation of the field boundaries at Blenheim Farm in Phase B cannot be precisely determined. The medieval activity here spans a period of demographic and economic upheaval which wrought its changes on the rural landscape of the region. The period of population expansion from the 11th to 13th centuries was halted by an agrarian crisis which had an early and severe impact on the Cotswolds. The population was already in decline before the Black Death of 1348–9 and the impact of shrinking and abandoned settlement had its effect on the upkeep and organisation of the surrounding farmland (Dyer 2002, 31). However, some individuals prospered as they took over other smallholdings and the refounded settlement at Moreton-in-Marsh may even have benefited from an incoming migration from the abandoned uplands.

The pottery assemblage suggests that manuring of arable land ceased in the first half of the 14th century. The latest pottery recovered from the site was associated with Building 1, which may have continued in occupation for a short period after the previous arable farming system had been abandoned. What is clear is that the small pens appear to have been rendered redundant at a time when one or more large fields were delineated, overlying the earlier enclosure ditches. The environmental evidence from Waterhole 2, which cuts through an earlier enclosure boundary, suggests domestic waste is present only in small quantities and insect species consistent with open areas and grassland are prevalent. The absence of charred plant remains in the sample from the hollow 2149 is a further indication that manuring had ceased. The inference from this is that a pastoral economy presides at this period, and the necessity to manage stock in small enclosures has been removed from this particular area by the provision of permanent pasture close at hand. A flock owned by a single individual that was provided with lowland pasture would not need to be counted and separated in the same way as animals belonging to several peasants after returning from more distant grazing.

The latest features to be ascribed to this period suggest continuing pastoral activity as Building 1 was abandoned and partially removed by a hollow feature, presumed to be formed by the passage of animals down to the stream. Later still in the sequence, this feature was replaced by a waterhole, to which livestock may have been driven to drink. The plant remains from the earlier of these two features includes woodland, scrub or hedgerow species. The absence of evidence for any human activity, other than the possible provision of a watering hole for livestock, suggests that the excavated area at Blenheim Farm had assumed a marginal status by this period and it is apparent from the location of the post-medieval field boundary that the medieval field ditches were no longer maintained.

The interpretations offered here attempt to set the excavated evidence within the known framework for the development of the medieval countryside in the Cotswolds. Our knowledge to date relies heavily on the work of landscape historians, most notably Christopher Dyer, who have proposed a model of medieval rural land-use based on an interdisciplinary approach combining documentary sources, earthwork survey and excavated evidence. Evidence of comparable sites remains sparse, particularly in the excavated record, and is still biased towards evidence preserved (often by earthwork remains) in areas that have maintained a more marginal status in the rural landscape following the agrarian crisis. A recent overview recognises there are 'yawning gaps' in our knowledge of the medieval rural archaeology of the region (Bowden 2006, 182). Sites such as Blenheim Farm provide data, including environmental evidence, which will make a vital contribution to our understanding of the period.

ACKNOWLEDGEMENTS

The excavation and this publication were funded by Crest Nicholson (Midlands) Limited. We are grateful to Brian Bull, Warren Jennens and latterly Mark Allen, all of Crest Nicholson, and Charles Parry of Gloucestershire County Council Archaeology Section for their assistance. The excavation was managed by Mary Alexander and led by Jonathan Hart with the assistance of Catherine Cservenka, Nick Corcos, Joss Davis, Derek Evans, Heather Hirons, Darran Muddiman, John Naylor, Kirsty Owen, Kelly Saunders, David Sabin, Jon Webster, Briege Williams and Nicholas Witchell. The post-excavation was managed by Annette Hancocks, and the illustrations were prepared by Lorna Gray, Liz Gardner and Jemma Elliot. E.R. McSloy would like to thank Roger Jacobi for his help in identifying sources of the flint. The text was edited by Annette Hancocks and Martin Watts. The authors would like to thank Christopher Dyer and Neil Holbrook for their invaluable comments on an early draft of the text. The project archives and finds will be deposited with Corinium Museum, Cirencester.

BIBLIOGRAPHY

Ashton, N. and Lewis, S. 2002 'Deserted Britain: declining populations in the British late Middle Pleistocene', *Antiquity* **76**, 388–96

Allen, T.G., Darvill, T.C., Green, L.S. and Jones, M.U. 1993 *Excavations at Roughground Farm, Lechlade, Gloucestershire: a prehistoric and Roman landscape* Thames Valley Landscapes: the Cotswold Water Park **1**, Oxford, Oxford Archaeological Unit/ Oxford University Committee for Archaeology

Baldwin, R.C. and O'Neil, H.E. 1958 'A medieval site at Chalk Hill, Temple Guiting, Gloucestershire, 1957', *Trans. Bristol Gloucestershire Archaeol. Soc.* **77**, 61–5

Barfield, M. and Hodder, M. 1987 'Burnt mounds as saunas, and the prehistory of bathing', *Antiquity* **61**, 370–9

Barrett, J.C. 1980 'The pottery of the Later Bronze Age in Lowland England', *Proc. Prehist. Soc.* **46**, 297–319

Barrett, J., Bradley, R., Bowden, M. and Mead, B. 1983 'South Lodge after Pitt-Rivers', *Antiquity* **57**, 193–204

Barrett, J., Bradley, R. and Green, M. 1991 *Landscape, monuments and society: the prehistory of Cranborne Chase* Cambridge, Cambridge University Press

Bennett, K.D. 1994 *Annotated catalogue of pollen and pteridophyte spores of the British Isles* Cambridge, University of Cambridge Department of Plant Sciences

Bowden, M. 2006 'The medieval countryside' in N. Holbrook and J. Juřica (eds) 2006, 167–87

Bradley, R. 1981 'Various styles of urn: cemeteries and settlement in Southern England c. 1400–1000 BC', in R. Chapman, I. Kinnes and K. Randsborg (eds) 1981, *The archaeology of death* Cambridge, Cambridge University Press, 93–104

Bradley, R. 1990 *The passage of arms* Cambridge, Cambridge University Press

Bronk Ramsey, C. 2005 *OxCal v3.10* http://c14.arch.ox.ac.uk/embed.php?File=oxcal. html (accessed 13 December 2007)

Brossler, A. 2001 'Reading Business Park: the results of phases 1 and 2', in J. Brück (ed.) 2001, 129–38

Brossler, A., Early, R. and Allen, C. 2004 *Green Park (Reading Business Park) Phase 2 excavations 1995: Neolithic and Bronze Age site* Thames Valley Landscapes **6**, Oxford, Oxford Archaeological Unit

Brown, A.G. 1982 'Human impact on the former floodplain woodlands of the Seven', in M. Bell and S. Limbrey (eds) 1982, *Archaeological aspects of woodland ecology* BAR Int. Ser. **146**, Oxford, British Archaeological Reports, 93–104

Brown, A.G, 1983 'Floodplain deposits and accelerated sedimentation in the lower Severn basin', in K.J. Gregory (ed.) 1983, *Background to palaeohydrology* Chichester, Wiley, 375–97

Brown, A.G. and Barber, K.E. 1985 'Late Holocene palaeoecology and sedimentary history of a small lowland catchment in central England', *Quaternary Research* **24**, 87–102

Brück, J. (ed.) 2001 *Bronze Age landscapes: tradition and transformation* Oxford, Oxbow Books

Burgess, C. 1980 *The Age of Stonehenge* London, Dent

CA (Cotswold Archaeology) 2005 'Blenheim Farm, Moreton-in-Marsh, Gloucestershire: post-excavation assessment and updated project design', CA unpublished report no. **04107**

CAT (Cotswold Archaeological Trust) 1997 'Blenheim Farm, Moreton-in-Marsh, Gloucestershire: archaeological evaluation', CAT unpublished report no. **97488**

Campbell, G. and Straker, V. 2003 'Prehistoric crop husbandry and plant use in southern England: development and regionality', in K.A. Robson Brown (ed.) 2003, 14–30

Carruthers, W.J. 2005 'The charred and waterlogged plant remains', in CA 2005, 48–54

Coates, G.A.C. (ed.) 2002 *Prehistoric and Romano-British landscape: excavations at Whitemoor Haye Quarry, Staffordshire, 1997–1999* BAR Brit. Ser. **340**, Oxford, British Archaeological Reports

Cowgill, J., DeNeergarad, M. and Griffiths, N. 1987 *Medieval finds from excavations in London, vol. 5: knives and scabbards* London, Museum of London/HMSO

Clifford, E. 1933 'The Roman villa, Hucclecote', *Trans. Bristol Gloucestershire Archaeol. Soc.* **55**, 323–36

Clifford, E. 1936 'A palaeolith found near Gloucester', *Antiq. J.* **16**, 91

Clifford, E. 1939 'Palaeolith from the upper Thames', *Antiq. J.* **19**, 193

Cracknell, S. 1988 'Bridge End, Warwick: archaeological excavation of a medieval street frontage', *Trans. Birmingham Warwickshire Archaeol. Soc.* **95**, 17–72

Cracknell, S. and Jones, M. 1985 'Medieval kiln debris from School Road, Alcester', *Trans. Birmingham Warwickshire Archaeol. Soc.* **94**, 107–22

Cracknell, S. and Mahany, C. 1994 *Roman Alcester: southern extramural area 1964–66 excavations. Part 2: finds and discussion* Roman Alcester vol. 1. CBA Res. Rep. **97**, York, Council for British Archaeology

Darvill, T. 1987 *Prehistoric Gloucestershire* Gloucester, Alan Sutton/Gloucestershire County Library

Darvill, T. 1988 'Excavations on the site of the Early Norman castle at Gloucester 1983–84', *Medieval Archaeol.* **32**, 1–49

Darvill, T. 2000 'Excavation in The Buckles', in E. Price 2000, 193–210

Darvill, T. 2006 'Early prehistory', in N. Holbrook and J. Juřica (eds) 2006, 5–60

Davis, S.J.M. 1992 *A rapid method for recording information about mammal bones from archaeological sites* Ancient Monuments Laboratory Rep. **19/92**

Dinn, J. and Evans, J. 1990 'Aston Mill Farm, Kemerton: excavation of a ring-ditch, Middle Iron Age enclosure and grubenhaus', *Trans. Worcestershire Archaeol. Soc. 3 ser.* **12**, 5–66

Douglas, T.D. 1980 'The Quaternary deposits of western Leicestershire', *Phil. Trans. Roy. Soc. London* **B288**, 259–86

Drewett, P. 1979. 'New evidence for the structure and function of Middle Bronze Age round houses in Sussex', *Arch. J.* **136**, 3–11

Dyer, C. 1995 'Sheepcotes: evidence for medieval farming', *Medieval Archaeol.* **39**, 136–64

Dyer, C. 1996 'Seasonal settlement in medieval Gloucestershire: sheepcotes', in H.S.A. Fox (ed.) 1996, 25–34

Dyer, C. 2002 'Villages and non-villages in the medieval Cotswolds', *Trans. Bristol Gloucestershire Archaeol. Soc.* **120**, 11–36

Edmonds, M. 1989 *Monument Protection Programme Monument Class Description: Martin Down Style Enclosures.* London, English Heritage [available online at www.eng-h.gov. uk/mpp/mcd/mcdtop1.htm (accessed 8 January 2008)]

Ellison, A. 1984 'Bronze Age Gloucestershire: artefacts and distributions', in A. Saville (ed.) 1984, 113–27

Evans, J. 1990 'The finds', in J. Dinn and J. Evans 1990, 26–39

FA (Framework Archaeology) 2006 *Landscape evolution in the middle Thames Valley. Heathrow Terminal 5 excavations vol. 1, Perry Oaks* FA Monograph **1**, Oxford and Salisbury, Framework Archaeology

Ford, D.A. 1995 *Medieval pottery in Staffordshire, AD 800–1600: a review* Staffordshire Archaeol. Stud. **7**, Stoke on Trent, City Museum and Art Gallery

Fox, H.S.A. (ed.) 1996 *Seasonal settlement* Vaughan Paper **39**, Leicester, University of Leicester Department of Adult Education

Gale, R. and Cutler, D. 2000 *Plants in archaeology* Kew, Westbury and Royal Botanic Gardens

Goodall, I.H. 1980 'Ironwork in medieval Britain: an archaeological study', unpublished PhD thesis, University of Cardiff

Greatorex, P.A. 1988 'The pottery', in T. Darvill 1988, 20–7

GSGB (Geological Survey Great Britain) 1981 *Geological survey of England and Wales, 1:50,000 series, Solid and Drift, map sheet 217: Moreton-in-Marsh* Southampton, Ordnance Survey

Hansen, M. 1987 *The Hydrophilidae (Coleoptera) of Fennoscandia and Denmark fauna* Fauna Entomologyca Scandinavica **18**, Leiden, Scandinavian Science Press

Hearne, C.M. and Heaton, M.J. 1994 'Excavations at a Late Bronze Age settlement in the Upper Thames Valley at Shorncote Quarry near Cirencester, 1992', *Trans. Bristol Gloucestershire Archaeol. Soc.* **52**, 17–58

Heighway, C. 1983 *The east and north gates of Gloucester* Western Archaeological Trust Excavation Monograph **4**, Bristol, Western Archaeological Trust

Hey, G. 1995 'Iron Age and Roman settlement at Old Shifford Farm, Standlake', *Oxoniensia* **LX**, 93–176

Hill, M.O., Mountford, J.O., Roy, D.B. and Bunce, R.G.H. 1999 *Ellenberg's indicator values for British plants* ECOFACT **2**, London, HMSO Technical Annex

Holbrook, N. and Juřica, J. (eds) 2006 *Twenty-Five Years of Archaeology in Gloucestershire. A review of new discoveries and new thinking in Gloucestershire, South Gloucestershire and Bristol* Bristol and Gloucestershire Archaeol. Rep. **3**, Cirencester, Cotswold Archaeology

Hurst, D. 1992 'Pottery', in S. Woodiwiss (ed.) 1992, 132–54

Jackson, R. and Napthan, M. 1998 'Interim report on salvage recording of a Neolithic/ Beaker and Bronze Age settlement and landscape at Huntsmans Quarry, Kemerton, 1996', *Trans. Worcestershire Archaeol. Soc. 3 ser.* **16**, 57–68

Jacomet, S. 1987 *Prähistorische Getreidefunde* Basle, Botanisches Institute der Universitut Abteilung Pflanzensystematik und Geobotanik

Jennings, D., Muir, J., Palmer, S. and Smith, A. 2004 *Thornhill Farm, Fairford, Gloucestershire: an Iron Age and Roman pastoral site in the Upper Thames Valley* Thames Valley Landscapes Monograph **23**, Oxford, Oxford Archaeology

Jones, M. 1981 'The development of crop husbandry', in M. Jones and G. Dimbleby (eds) 1981, 95–121

Jones, M. (ed.) 1983 *Integrating the subsistence economy* BAR Int. Ser. **181**, Oxford, British Archaeological Reports

Jones, M. and Dimbleby, G. (eds) 1981 *The Environment of Man: the Iron Age to the Anglo-Saxon Period* BAR Brit. Ser. **87**, Oxford, British Archaeological Reports

Jope, E.M. 1952 'Medieval pottery', in H. O'Neil 1952, 61–76

Keen, D.H. and Bridgland, D.R. 1986 'An interglacial fauna from Avon no. 3 Terrace at Eckington, Worcestershire', *Proc. Geol. Ass.* **97**, 303–7

Kenward, H.K., Hall, A.R. and Jones, A.K.G. 1980 'A tested set of techniques for the extraction of plant and animal macrofossils from waterlogged archaeological deposits', *Sci. and Archaeol.* **22**, 3–15

Lambrick, G. 1988 *The Rollright Stones. Megaliths, monuments and settlement in the prehistoric landscape* HBMCE Report **6**, London, English Heritage

Lang, A.T.O. and Keen, D.H. 2005 'At the edge of the world… Hominid colonisation and the Lower and Middle Palaeolithic of the West Midlands', *Proc. Prehist. Soc.* **71**, 63–84

Langton, B., Ings, M., Walker, G. and Oakey, N. 2000 'Medieval field systems at Tinker's Close, Moreton-in-Marsh, Gloucestershire: excavations in 1995–1996', in N. Oakey (ed.) 2000, 15–23

Leah, M. and Young, C. 2001 'A Bronze Age burnt mound at Sandy Lane, Charlton Kings, Gloucestershire: excavations in 1971', *Trans. Bristol Gloucestershire Archaeol. Soc.* **119**, 59–82

Leech, R. 1981 *Historic towns in Gloucestershire* Gloucester, Committee for Rescue Archaeology in Avon, Gloucestershire and Somerset

Lindroth, C.H. 1974 *Coleoptera: Carabidae* Handbooks for the Identification of British Insects **4/2**, London, Royal Entomological Society of London

Lucht, W.H. 1987 *Die Käfer Mitteleuropas (Katalog)* Krefeld, Goecke and Evers

McKinley, J.L. 1993 'Bone fragment size and weights of bone from modern British cremation and implications for the interpretation of archaeological cremations', *Int. J. Osteoarchaeol.* **3**, 283–7

Mellor, M. 1994 'A synthesis of Middle and Late Saxon, medieval and early post-medieval pottery in the Oxford region', *Oxoniensia* **59**, 17–217

Moore, J. and Jennings, D. 1992 *Reading Business Park: a Bronze Age landscape* Thames Valley Landscapes: the Kennet Valley **1**, Oxford, Oxford Archaeological Unit

Moore, P.D., Webb, J.A. and Collinson, M.E. 1991 *Pollen analysis* Oxford, Blackwell Scientific Publications

Morris, E. 1980 'Medieval and post-medieval pottery in Worcester: a type series', *Trans. Worcestershire. Archaeol. Soc. 3 ser.* **7**, 221–53

Needham, S. 1996 'Chronology and periodization in the British Bronze Age', in K. Randsborg (ed.) 1996, *Absolute chronology. Archaeological Europe 2500–500 BC* Act Archaeologica **67** and Acta Archaeologica Supplementa **I**, Copenhagen, Munksgaard, 121–40

Needham, S., Bronk Ramsay, C., Coombs, D., Cartwright, C. and Pettitt, P. 1997 'An independent chronology for British Bronze Age metalwork: the results of the Oxford Radiocarbon Accelerator Programme', *Arch. J.* 154, 55–107

Neville Terry, W. 1953 'A bronze spear-head from Moreton-in-Marsh', *Trans. Bristol Gloucestershire Archaeol. Soc.* **72**, 150–1

Nilsson, A.N. and Holmen, M. 1995 *The aquatic Adephaga (Coleoptera) of Fennoscandia and Denmark II. Dytiscidae* Fauna Entomologica Scandinavica **32**, Leiden and Copenhagen, Scandinavian Science Press

Nowakowski, J. 1991 'Trethellan Farm, Newquay: the excavation of a lowland Bronze Age settlement and Iron Age cemetery', *Cornish Archaeol.* **30**, 5–242

Oakey, N. (ed.) 2000 Three medieval sites in Gloucestershire: Excavations at Westward Road, Ebley; Tinker's Close, Moreton-in-Marsh; and Maidenhill, Stonehouse 1995–1998 CAT Occas. Pap. **1**, Cirencester, Cotswold Archaeological Trust

O'Neil, H. 1952 'Whittington Court Roman Villa, Whittington, Gloucestershire: a report of the excavations undertaken from 1948 to 1951', *Trans. Bristol Gloucestershire Archaeol. Soc.* **71**, 13–87

O'Neil, H. 1967 'Bevan's Quarry round barrow, Temple Guiting, 1964', *Trans. Bristol Gloucestershire Archaeol. Soc.* **86**, 16–41

Payne, S. 1973 'Kill-off patterns in sheep and goats: the mandibles from Asvan Kale', *Anatolian Stud.* **23**, 281–303

Peacock, D.P.S. (ed.) 1977 *Pottery and early commerce. Characterization and trade in Roman and later ceramics* London, Academic Press

Piggott, C.M. 1942 'Five late Bronze Age enclosures in north Wiltshire', *Proc. Prehist. Soc.* **8**, 48–61

Pine, J. and Preston, S. 2004 *Iron Age and Roman settlement and landscape at Totterdown Lane, Horcott, near Fairford, Gloucestershire* TVAS Monograph **6**, Reading, Thames Valley Archaeological Services

Price, E. 2000 *Frocester: a Romano-British settlement, its antecedents and successors vol. 1: The Sites* Stonehouse, Gloucester and District Archaeological Research Group

Rahtz, P. and ApSimon, A. 1962 'Excavations at Shearplace Hill, Sydling St Nicholas, Dorset, England', *Proc. Prehist. Soc.* **28**, 289–328

Rátkai, S. 1988 'The medieval pottery', in S. Cracknell 1988, 33–58

Rátkai, S. 1994 'Medieval pottery', in S. Cracknell and C. Mahany 1994, 154–6

RCHME (Royal Commission on the Historic Monuments of England) 1976 *Ancient and historical monuments in the county of Gloucestershire vol. 1: Iron Age and Roman monuments in the Gloucestershire Cotswolds* London, HMSO

Reimer, P.J., Baillie, M.G.L., Bard, E., Bayliss, A., Beck, J.W., Bertrand, C., Blackwell, P.G., Buck, C.E., Burr, G., Cutler, K.B., Damon, P.E., Edwards, R.L., Fairbanks, R.G., Friedrich, M., Guilderson, T.P., Hughen, K.A., Kromer, B., McCormac, F.G., Manning, S., Bronk Ramsey, C., Reimer, R.W., Remmele, S., Southon, J.R., Stuiver, M., Talamo, S., Taylor, F.W., van der Plicht, J. and Weyhenmeyer, C.E. 2004 'IntCal04 terrestrial radiocarbon age calibration, 0–26 cal kyr BP', *Radiocarbon* **46** (3), 1029–58

Robinson, M.A. 1981 'The use of ecological groupings of Coleoptera for comparing sites', in M. Jones and G. Dimbleby (eds) 1981, 251–86

Robinson, M.A. 1983 'Arable/pastoral ratios from insects?', in M. Jones (ed.) 1983, 19–47

Robson Brown, K.A. (ed.) 2003 *Archaeological sciences 1999: proceedings of the Archaeological Sciences Conference, University of Bristol, 1999* BAR International series 1111, Oxford, Archaeopress

Roe, D.A. 1981 *The lower and middle Palaeolithic periods in Britain* London, Routledge

Saville, A. 1983 'Excavations at Condicote henge monument, Gloucestershire, 1977', *Trans. Bristol Gloucestershire Archaeol. Soc.* **101**, 21–48

Saville, A. (ed.) 1984 *Archaeology in Gloucestershire* Cheltenham, Cheltenham Art Gallery and Museums/Bristol and Gloucestershire Archaeological Society

Shaffrey, R. 2003 'The rotary querns from the Society of Antiquaries' excavations at Silchester, 1890–1909', *Britannia* **34**, 143–74

Smith, D.N. 1999 'The insect remains from Covert Farm (DIRFT East), Crick, Northamptonshire', unpublished report for Birmingham University Field Archaeology Unit

Smith, D.N. 2002 'The insect remains', in G.A.C. Coates 2002, 67–72

Stace, C. 1991 *New flora of the British Isles* Cambridge, Cambridge University Press

Stace, C. 1997 *New flora of the British Isles* (2nd edition) Cambridge, Cambridge University Press

Stallybrass, S. and Huntley, J.P. (eds) 2000 *Taphonomy and interpretation* Oxford, Oxbow

Stone, J.F.S. 1936 'An enclosure on Boscombe Down East', *Wiltshire Archaeol. Natur. Hist. Mag.* **47**, 466–89

Stuiver, M. and Polach, H.A. 1977 'Discussion: Reporting of 14C Data', *Radiocarbon* **19** (3), 355–63

Stuiver, M. and Reimer, P.J. 1993 'Extended 14C database and revised CALIB 3.0 14C age calibration program', *Radiocarbon* **35** (1), 215–30

Sumbler, M.G. 2001 'The Moreton Drift: a further clue to glacial chronology in central England', *Proc. Geol. Ass.* **112**, 13–27

Thomas, A., Holbrook, N. and Bateman, C. 2003 *Later Prehistoric and Romano-British burial and settlement at Hucclecote, Gloucestershire* Bristol and Gloucestershire Archaeol. Rep. **2**, Cirencester, Cotswold Archaeology

Timby, J.R. 1998 *Excavations at Kingscote and Wycombe, Gloucestershire* Cirencester, Cotswold Archaeological Trust

Timby, J.R. 2000 'The pottery', in B. Langton *et al.* 2000, 18–21

Timby, J.R. 2003 'The pottery', in A. Thomas *et al.* 2003, 31–44

Timby, J.R. 2004 'Prehistoric pottery', in G. Walker *et al.* 2004, 59–62

Tipping, R. 2000 'Pollen preservation analysis as a necessity in Holocene palynology', in S. Stallybrass and J.P. Huntley (eds) 2000, 22–34

Tomber, R. and Dore, J. 1998 *The National Roman Fabric Reference Collection: a handbook* London, Museum of London Archaeology Service

Vince, A.G. 1977 'The medieval and post-medieval ceramic industry of the Malvern region: the study of its ware and distribution', in D.P.S. Peacock (ed.) 1977, 257–305

Vince, A.G. 1983 'The medieval pottery', in C. Heighway 1983, 125–31

Vince, A.G. 1984 'Late Saxon and medieval pottery in Gloucestershire', in A. Saville (ed.) 1984, 248–75

Vince, A.G. 2003 'Prehistoric fabrics', in A. Thomas *et al.* 2003, 32–3

Walker, G., Thomas, A. and Bateman, C. 2004 'Bronze Age and Romano-British sites south-east of Tewkesbury: evaluations and excavations 1991–7', *Trans. Bristol Gloucestershire Archaeol. Soc.* **122**, 29–94

Watts, L. and Rahtz, P. 1985 *Mary-le-Port Bristol: excavations 1962/3* City of Bristol Museum and Art Gallery Monograph **7**, Bristol, City of Bristol Museum and Art Gallery

Weaver, S. 2004 'Somerford Keynes, Shorncote, Cotswold Community', *Trans. Bristol Gloucestershire Archaeol. Soc.* **122**, 187–8

Wilkinson, K. and Stevens, S. 2003 *Environmental archaeology: approaches, techniques and applications* Stroud, Tempus

Woodward, A. 1998 'The pottery', in R. Jackson and M. Napthan 1998, 63–5

Woodiwiss, S. (ed.) 1992 *Iron Age and Roman salt production and the medieval town of Droitwich. Excavations at the Old Bowling Green and Friar Street* CBA Res. Rep. **81**, London, Council for British Archaeology

PREHISTORIC AND MEDIEVAL REMAINS AT 21 CHURCH ROAD, BISHOP'S CLEEVE: EXCAVATIONS IN 2004

by Kate Cullen and Annette Hancocks

with contributions by
Wendy J. Carruthers, E.R. McSloy, Sylvia Warman and Martin Watts

INTRODUCTION

Numerous archaeological investigations have been made and reported on at Bishop's Cleeve over the last 15 years, with evidence for Iron Age, Romano-British, Late Saxon and medieval activity recorded. The current site (SO 9587 2769: Fig. 1) lies immediately to the south of Gilder's Paddock, where Iron Age, Romano-British and medieval occupation was uncovered in 1989/90 (Parry 1999). Further occupation is attested to the south of Church Road, now Tesco supermarket (Lovell *et al.* 2007), and to the west at Home Farm (Barber and Walker 1998) and Stoke Road (Enright and Watts 2002).

A planning application for residential development of 21 Church Road was submitted to Tewkesbury Borough Council, which requested an archaeological evaluation to inform the planning process. This evaluation indicated that medieval and post-medieval remains survived within the proposed development area (CA 2003). Planning permission was subsequently granted with an archaeological condition attached that required an excavation and a watching brief to be undertaken. This work was carried out in April/May and November 2004 by Cotswold Archaeology. The results of the evaluation, the excavation and watching brief are reported here.

Topography and geology

The site is within the historic core of the village, at approximately 55m AOD and 200m south-west of the Late Norman church of St Michael and All Angels. Prior to excavation the site comprised a bakery fronting Church Road to the south, with car parking to the side and rear, and a small raised garden, about 1m above the level of the car park, at its northern end. Excavation was undertaken within the car park and garden.

The underlying geology of the area is mapped as Cheltenham Sand of the Quaternary period (GSGB 1981). The natural substrate encountered throughout the excavation area comprised sands and occasional gravel deposits.

Excavation methodology

The excavations were carried out in accordance with a brief prepared by Gloucestershire County Council and comprised the excavation of an area measuring approximately 20m by 45m, and a subsequent watching brief during the demolition of garages on the eastern side of the site (Figs 1 and 2). The topsoil and subsoil were removed by mechanical excavator to a depth of 0.65m in the raised garden area, which sloped slightly downwards to the south. In

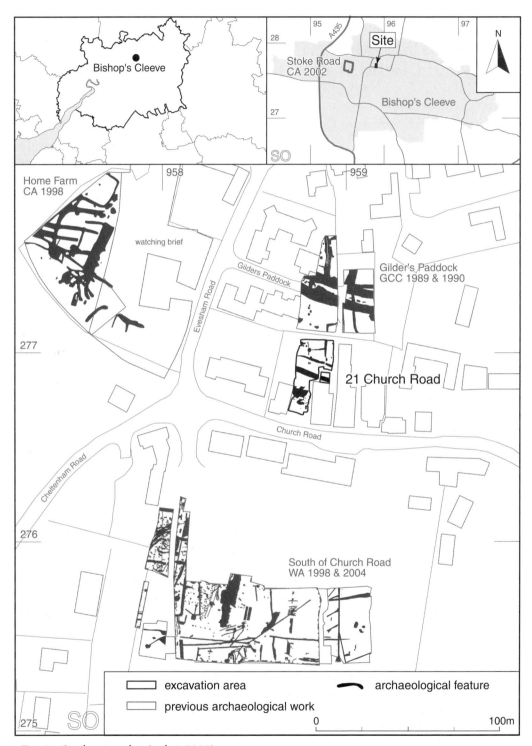

Fig. 1: Site location plan (scale 1:2000)

contrast, only 0.3m of car park surface and overburden was removed from the southern part of the site, resulting in a 0.65m difference in height between excavation levels to either side of the retained modern wall. Archaeological remains survived as cut features, stone walls and surfaces. Hand excavation of at least 50% of all discrete features and of at least 20% of all linear features then followed. The total area of excavation was 850m^2.

EXCAVATION RESULTS

Archaeological features and deposits were encountered across the excavation area (Fig. 2), including ditches, gullies, pits, postholes and structures. Artefactual material was retrieved from the majority of features, which enabled five broad periods of activity to be identified:

Period 1: Iron Age
Period 2: Roman/Early Saxon
Period 3: Medieval
Period 4: Post-medieval
Period 5: Modern

Features and/or artefacts attributed to the first four periods are described below. Modern deposits and features, which included 19th-century stone tanks or cisterns, brick and cobbled yard surfaces and associated construction horizons, and 20th-century service trenches and layers of demolition debris, are not reported on. Full details can be found in the project archive.

Period 1: Iron Age (Figs 2–3)

Evidence of Iron Age activity comprising pits, gullies and ditches was found across the northern half of the site. Most of the features assigned to this period contained a few sherds of Iron Age pottery.

Five intercutting pits were identified in the north-western corner of the site (Pit Group 1). These covered an area approximately 2m in diameter and extended beyond the limit of excavation. The two earliest pits (1146, 1149) were both 0.65m deep, with flat bases and steep or undercut sides (Fig. 3, Section 2), and were subcircular in plan with diameters of 0.65m and 1.2m. Their form suggests that their original function was for grain storage. They contained a few large and unabraded pottery sherds, fired-clay objects and bones from cattle and sheep/goat. The later pits (1154, 1155, 1159) were shallower and more irregular, and their function was unclear, although their fills were similar to those of the earlier pits. Close by were two more pits (Pit Group 2). These were both circular in plan, 0.9m in diameter and up to 0.35m in depth (Fig. 3, Section 3). These pits also may have been for grain storage. Pit 1008 contained several pottery sherds, and a fragment of a blue-and-white glass bead of probable Iron Age date (Fig. 5).

To the east of the pits, two gullies and a ditch formed an 'H' arrangement (Fig. 2). Gully 1 was orientated east/west, was between 0.3m and 0.85m wide with a rounded profile, and survived to a depth of 0.3m (Fig. 3, Section 4). At the western end of Gully 1 was Gully 2, of similar dimensions but aligned north/south. Its northern end could not be clearly

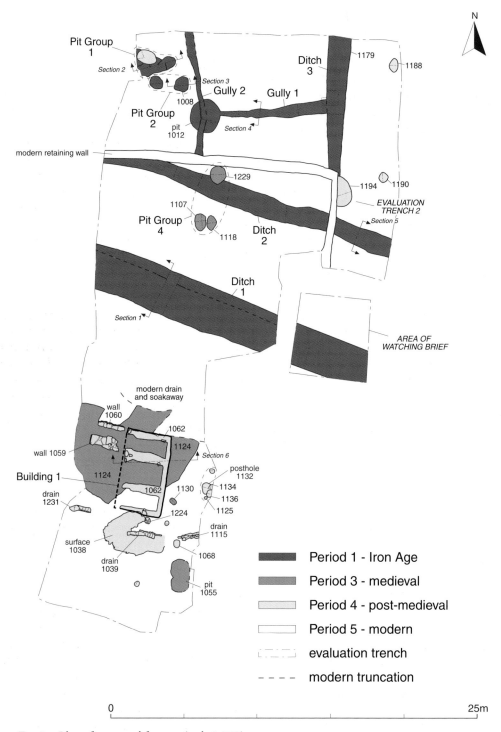

Fig. 2: Plan of excavated features (scale 1:250)

traced, and it was truncated by the car park terracing to the south. At their intersection was a large circular pit (1012), 2m in diameter and 0.65m deep, which contained fragments of pottery and animal bone. The relationships between these features were not certain, although Gully 2 may have been later than pit 1012; if so, the pit may have acted as a soakaway, with Gully 1 channelling rainwater into it. Gully 1 did not extend eastwards beyond its intersection with north/south-aligned Ditch 3, a more substantial feature of up to 1.1m width and 0.25m depth. Like Gully 2, Ditch 3 continued to the north of the excavation area and was truncated by terracing to the south.

To the south of the raised garden area were Ditches 1 and 2, both aligned north-west/south-east. Terracing had removed any evidence for relationships between these ditches and those features to the north. Ditch 1 was 3m wide by 1.2m deep, and had been recut at least once. The primary ditch, 1090, was undated, but a fill (1084) of the recut contained several fragments of animal bone and pottery (Fig. 3, Section 1). Ditch 2 was parallel to and 5.5m to the north of Ditch 1. Ditch 2 had been truncated greatly by the terracing, but to the east, where it survived better, it was over 0.5m deep (Fig. 3, Section 5) and contained a small number of pottery sherds and animal bone fragments. Ditches 1 and 2 presumably defined a broad track or droveway.

Dating evidence

Dating evidence for Period 1 is provided primarily by the pottery, with fabrics and forms corresponding to larger assemblages from the Gloucestershire region including Gilder's Paddock (Hancocks 1999, 105) and Crickley Hill (Elsdon 1994, 213–41). A broad chronological distinction is discernable. Pit Group 1 produced earlier or Middle Iron Age forms in fossil shell/limestone-tempered fabrics, whereas material from pit 1012 and the gullies and ditches consisted of Late Iron Age Malvernian-type fabrics. A glass bead from the primary fill of pit 1008 (Pit Group 2) dates to the Middle to Late Iron Age. The assemblage has close parallels and affinities with the pottery fabrics and forms of Middle Iron Age date recovered from Pit Groups 1 and 2, and features 46/220 and 47/210, at Gilder's Paddock (Parry 1999, 99).

Period 2: Roman and Saxon

This period is only represented by 31 residual sherds of pottery (Tables 1–2) retrieved from later medieval pits. The absence of Roman and Saxon features on the site suggests a lack of continuity of settlement within the site, although not necessarily within the general locality.

Period 3: Medieval (Figs 2–4)

This period was represented mainly by pits. The main focus of activity was to the south of (Iron Age) Ditch 1, but three pits (Pit Group 4) lay to the north of Ditch 1. Two of these pits, 1107 and 1229, contained the partially articulated remains of horses; pit 1229 also contained a single fragment of medieval pottery as well as residual sherds of Roman and Saxon pottery (see above). Pit 1107 was 0.7m in diameter and 0.3m deep, while pit 1229 was larger at 1.1m in diameter and over 0.5m deep. The third pit, 1118, was undated but comparable in size, and adjacent to, pit 1107, suggesting it was contemporary.

In the southern part of the site there were at least 17 intercutting pits (Pit Group 3; Fig. 3, Section 6). The pits varied in shape but most were subcircular, up to 2.7m in diameter

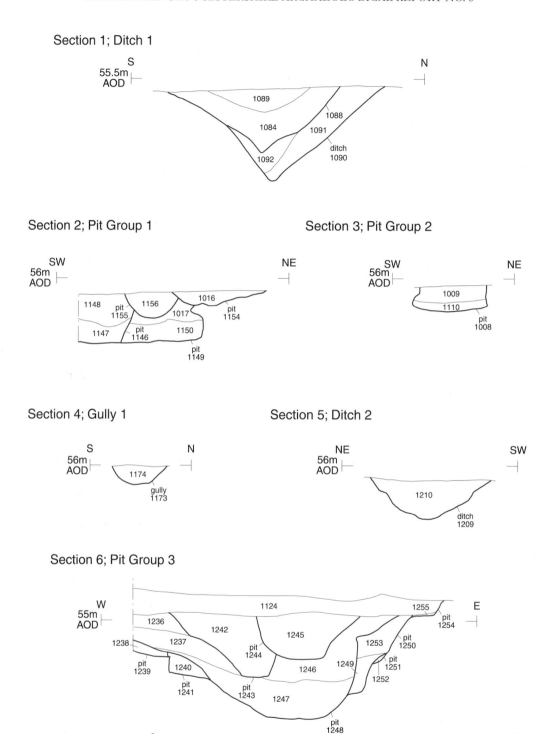

Fig. 3: Sections 1 to 6 (scale 1:50)

with concave bases, and several had undercut sides. Their primary function may have been storage, but the recovery of a large quantity of medieval pottery and animal bone, including a partially articulated dog skeleton from pit 1205 (not illustrated), indicates the pits were later used for the disposal of domestic waste, and for a possible pet burial. Sixteen sherds of residual Saxon pottery were also recovered from this pit group. In the south-east corner of the site was a large pit, 1055, approximately 2.5m in diameter and 1.3m in depth, with undercut edges. Originally it may have been stone-lined as it contained several large limestone fragments. As with Pit Group 3, the pit seems to have been used ultimately for the disposal of domestic waste. After Pit Group 3 went out of use a 0.12m-thick dark soil layer (1124) formed, most probably as a result of ploughing (Fig. 3, Section 6).

Dating evidence

Pit Group 4 is dated by a single sherd of Cotswold-type pottery from pit 1229, dating to the 11th to 13th century, while Pit Group 3 is dated by 153 medieval sherds, including a sherd from a tripod pitcher in a glazed Worcester fabric from the mid 12th to mid 13th century. Pit 1055 contained Malvernian and Cotswold-type pottery of 12th to 14th-century date, in forms such as simple and developed everted rimmed jars. The cultivation layer 1124 contained pottery of a similar date range (12th to 13th century). There are few elements, such as imported tableware forms, which might permit closer dating or relative ceramic phasing. Aspects of the Period 3 pottery, such as the proportions of Cotswold and Malvern cooking-pot fabrics, the prevalence of developed rim forms and the occurrence of wheel-finished Malvern jar rims, suggest that most material dates to between the mid 12th to mid 13th century.

Period 4: Post-medieval (Fig. 2)

Apart from four pits at the northern end of the site, evidence for post-medieval activity was restricted to the southern third of the site and included the remains of a small building with a cobbled surface and drain, and a number of postholes.

The remains of Building 1 comprised four parallel robber trenches, with a fifth robber trench at the eastern end (all trench 1062), all of which contained the same rubble infill. The robbed walls were probably foundations for a raised rectangular structure, approximately 5m by 3m (Fig. 2). To the west, two parallel stone walls (1059 and 1060) survived up to two courses high. Wall 1059 was 0.7m wide whereas wall 1060 was 0.35m wide, but both were aligned with Building 1 and may have supported steps up to it. Pottery dating from the 11th to 13th century was retrieved from a deposit associated with the construction of wall 1059, but this was probably residual from soil layer 1124, through which the foundation trenches had been dug. A token dating to 1690 and a bone-handled iron knife of probable 18th-century date were recovered from the rubble fill of robber trench 1062.

To the south were the remains of an undated cobbled surface (1038), which was probably associated with Building 1, although no direct evidence survived. Running east/west across surface 1038 was one of three heavily truncated sections of a stone drain (1039), with the two other surviving sections to the west (1231) and east (1115). Pottery associated with the construction of the drain dated from the 13th or 14th century, and this was also considered to be residual. A buckle, probably dating to the later 16th or 17th century, was retrieved from deposit 1167 (not illustrated) from within drain 1115. This deposit spread well beyond drain 1115, and was cut by the southernmost part of robber trench 1062.

A number of postholes were situated around the eastern and southern sides of Building 1, but there was no coherent pattern to indicate their function. Ten postholes were excavated, varying in size from 0.2m to 0.55m in diameter and from 0.2m to 0.4m in depth. Three of the ten postholes, 1132, 1134 and 1136, appeared to be intercutting. Pottery sherds dating from the 18th century were recovered from postholes 1132, 1068 and 1224. Four pits at the northern end of the site also yielded pottery dating to the 17th or 18th century.

THE FINDS
by E.R. McSloy

The pottery

Analysis of the pottery was confined to Periods 1 to 3. A small quantity of post-medieval pottery was also recovered from Period 4 features, largely utilitarian coarseware types from Malvern Chase or Staffordshire, for the most part dateable to between the 16th and 18th centuries (Table 1). Small quantities of tableware included tin-glazed earthenwares, most probably from Bristol, and stonewares from the Rhineland.

Fabric codes for Iron Age material are those utilised at the adjoining Gilder's Paddock site (Hancocks 1999, 104–5). Codes for later material conform to those used for Roman to medieval groups at Home Farm (Timby 1998, 126–8) and Stoke Road, Bishop's Cleeve (Timby 2002, 22–6), which incorporate nomenclature of the *National Roman Fabric Reference Collection* (Tomber and Dore 1998) and Gloucester City Museum (see Vince 1983).

Pottery fabrics were identified macroscopically or with the use of x20 binocular microscope. Recording was by minimum vessel and sherd counts, weight and rim estimated vessel equivalents (EVEs). Preservation of the stratified pottery was good with little abrasion or weathering noted. Average sherd weight for the small Iron Age group is very high at 23g, the effect of joining sherds from pit 1149, fills 1017 and 1150 (Pit Group 1; Fig. 3, Section 2).

Period 1: Iron Age
The Iron Age pottery (Tables 1–2) falls into two well-defined fabric groups, which almost certainly reflect differing chronology. The larger group from Pit Group 1 consists mainly of fossil shell/limestone-tempered fabric 3; significantly, Malvernian-type fabrics are absent. Identifiable forms include a slack-shouldered jar (Fig. 4.1) of Early or earlier Middle Iron Age date, and four Middle Iron Age-type barrel jars (Fig. 4.2–4). The second group, consisting of material from linear features and pit 1012 (Table 2: 'other features'), comprises Malvernian type B1, local limestone or quartz-tempered fabrics. No forms were identifiable among this group but the relative prominence of the Malvernian material, particularly the limestone-tempered type, probably indicates a Late Iron Age date.

The small Iron Age assemblage corresponds closely in terms of fabric range and broad chronology to the Iron Age material from Gilder's Paddock (Hancocks 1999, 105). The slack-shouldered jar with high neck and expanded rim from pit 1149 (Pit Group 1, Fig. 4.1) is close to a number of vessels from there (ibid., nos 28 and 31–2) and examples of Early Iron Age date from Crickley Hill (Elsdon 1994, 204). This vessel came from the basal fill of the earliest of a sequence of pits; the later fills of Pit Group 1 produced examples

Table 1: Pottery quantification by fabric, all periods

Fabric codes relate to previously published Iron Age material (Hancocks 1999), the Gloucester City Museum fabric type series (Vince 1983) and to the *National Roman Fabric Reference Collection* (Tomber and Dore 1998).

Description	Fabric Code	Count	Weight (g)	Min. vess.	EVEs
Period 1: Iron Age					
Malvernian rock-tempered (Peacock 1968, A)	1	1	3	1	-
Malvernian limestone-tempered (Peacock 1968, B1)	2	5	69	3	-
Local fossil-shell/limestone-tempered	3	19	568	13	.29
Quartz-tempered	5	3	12	3	-
Sub-total		28	652	20	.29
Period 2: Roman					
Severn Valley ware	SVW OX2	6	39	6	-
Oxfordshire red colour-coated	OXF RS	2	7	2	-
Local greyware	LOC GW	2	52	2	-
Local imitation BB	LOC IMBB	1	20	1	-
Malvernian wheel-thrown	MAL RT	1	10	1	.04
Sub-total		12	128	12	.04
Period 2: Anglo-Saxon					
Organic-tempered	SAX ORG	7	37	7	-
Quartz-tempered	SAX QZ	7	23	7	.02
Quartz with limestone	SAX QZLS	3	20	2	-
Quartz with organic	SAX QZORG	2	62	2	-
Sub-total		19	142	18	.02
Period 3: medieval					
Cotswold oolitic	TF41	64	685	47	.59
Malvern Chase cooking pot	TF40	102	1258	63	.78
Worcester? sandy	TF42	19	251	23	.27
Quartz and limestone	TF43	12	78	12	-
Minety ware	TF44	4	79	4	-
Malvern Chase glazed	TF52	4	39	3	-
Worcester glazed	TF90	3	121	3	-
Sub-total		208	2511	155	1.64
Period 4: post-medieval					
Malvernian redware	TF52	18	437	12	.15
Fine, micaceous (Newent Glasshouse?)	TF54	1	188	1	-
Tin glazed (Bristol/Staffs)	TF62	4	38	2	-
Frechen stoneware	TF68C	2	46	1	-
Yellow slipware (Bristol/Staffs)	TF72	1	4	1	-
Staffs Black-glazed earthenware	TF75	2	37	2	-
Unsourced glazed red earthenware	-	1	6	1	-
Sub-total		29	756	20	.15
Total		**296**	**4189**	**225**	**2.14**

Table 2: Pottery by Period and feature group, Periods 1 and 3

Period	Feature	Fabric	Count	Weight (g)	Min. vess.
1: Iron Age	Pit Group 1	3	17	562	12
		5	1	3	1
	Other features	1	1	3	1
		2	5	69	3
		3	2	6	1
		5	2	9	2
3: Medieval	Pit Group 3	LOC BB	1	20	1
		LOC GW	2	52	2
		MAL RT	1	10	1
		SVW OX2	4	28	4
		SAX ORG	7	37	7
		SAX QZ	6	21	6
		SAX QZLS	1	4	1
		SAX QZORG	2	62	2
		TF40	68	908	50
		TF41	50	522	33
		TF42	18	226	18
		TF43	9	43	8
		TF44	3	73	3
		TF52	2	14	1
		TF90	3	121	3
	Pit Group 4	OXF RS	1	2	1
		SAX QZLS	2	16	1
		SAX QZ	1	2	1
		TF41	1	1	1
	Building 1	TF40	20	231	3
		TF41	2	23	2
		TF43	1	19	1
		TF44	1	6	1
	Pit 1055	OXF RS	1	5	1
		SVW OX2	1	4	1
		TF41	10	125	10
		TF40	7	52	3
		TF42	1	25	5
Total			**254**	**3304**	**191**

of barrel jars of distinctively Middle Iron Age type. Overall the pottery conforms to the regional pattern, which experienced an increasing dominance of 'traded' wares in the Late Iron Age period (Ford and Rees forthcoming).

Period 2: Roman and Anglo-Saxon

Small quantities of Roman and Anglo-Saxon pottery were recovered (Table 1), all of which were residual within Period 3 features (Table 2). Roman material consists of local-type fabrics well known from other sites in Bishop's Cleeve, including Home Farm (Timby 1998, 126–8) and Stoke Road (Timby 2002, 22–6). Sherds of Oxfordshire red colour-coated ware and a late form of Severn Valley ware tankard (Webster 1976) suggest 3rd to 4th-century AD dating, which is in accordance with previously excavated stratified groups.

Anglo-Saxon pottery, all of which is handmade, is also comparable in terms of the range of fabrics to material recovered from elsewhere in Bishop's Cleeve (Timby 1998, 134; 2002, 22–6), and a similarly broad *c.* 5th to 9th-century AD date range can be assigned. No rims or decorated sherds were recovered, although joining sherds from Pit Group 3 derive from a mid-size globular-bodied vessel. Though residual, 16 of the 19 Anglo-Saxon sherds were recovered from Pit Group 3 and the unabraded condition of this group, its spatial coherence and the presence of cross-context joins, suggests that this material was disturbed from stratified deposits nearby.

Period 3: medieval

Medieval pottery accounts for the larger part of the assemblage (Table 1), much of which was recovered from Pit Group 3 (Table 2). The medieval assemblage consists predominantly of coarse 'cooking-pot' fabrics of two distinct classes: Malvern Chase ware (TF40) and oolitic limestone-tempered types (TF41 and TF43), probably from the Gloucester area. Sandy coarseware type (TF42) is unsourced but possibly derives from the Worcester area together with glazed type TF90. Other glazed tableware types comprise material from Malvern Chase (TF52) and Minety, north Wiltshire (TF44). The assemblage compares in some respects with the much larger group from Stoke Road (Timby 2002, 27–32). A significant difference, and one which probably relates to chronology, is the proportionally much greater incidence (30% by vessel count) of oolitic limestone-tempered Cotswold-type fabrics (TF41). The greater abundance of Cotswold-type fabrics and other aspects of the assemblage suggest that the bulk of the pottery dates to the mid 12th to mid 13th centuries. A possible (earlier) exception is a small group of pottery from pit 1229 (Pit Group 4). A single sherd of Cotswold type TF41 from this feature provides a 10th to 13th-century *terminus post quem*.

Vessel forms among the medieval pottery are largely confined to jars, with 'developed' everted-rims probably implying dating after *c.* AD 1150. Single examples of the earlier 'clubbed' and simple everted-jar rims are present among the Cotswold oolitic (TF41) material, although these are residual. The only medieval vessel illustrated (Fig. 4.5) is a typical Malvernian straight-sided jar with sagging base. Aside from cooking-pot types, few other forms were identifiable. A sherd tentatively identified as a glazed Worcester product from pit 1250 (Pit Group 3), but which is of an untypically coarse fabric, features decoration in the form of a wavy applied strip and comb stabbing. It is handmade and probably derives from a tripod pitcher of 12th to earlier 13th-century date (Bryant 2004, 297).

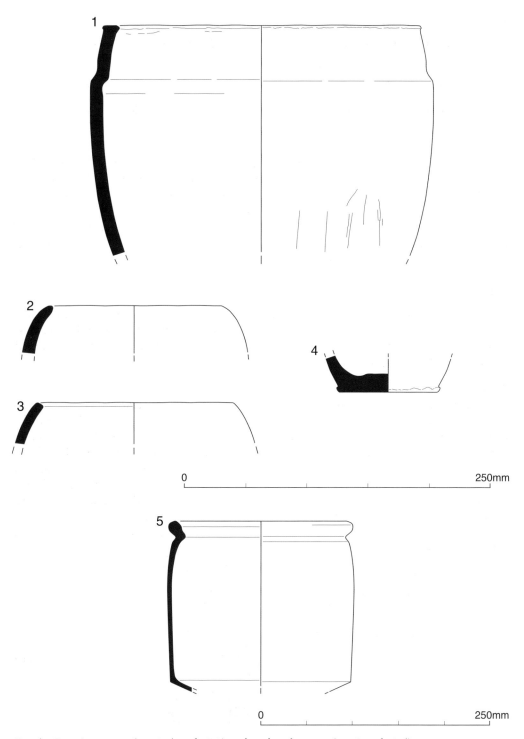

Fig. 4: Iron Age pottery (nos 1–4; scale 1:3) and medieval pottery (no. 5; scale 1:4)

Catalogue of illustrated sherds (Fig. 4)

1   Slack-shouldered jar with upright neck and expanded rim. Fabric 3. Period 2, Pit Group 1, Pit 1149, primary fill 1150.
2   Barrel jar with inturned, plain rim. Fabric 3. Fill 1009 of pit 1008, Pit Group 2, Period 2.
3   Barrel jar with inturned, plain rim. Fabric 3. Fill 1017 of pit 1149, Pit Group 1, Period 2.
4   'Pushed-out' base from ?jar. Fabric 3. Fill 1160 of pit 1159, Pit Group 1, Period 2.
5   Straight-sided jar with developed everted rim. Fabric TF40. Fill 1065 of trench 1064, Period 3.

The token

A single token was recovered from robber trench 1062. This is an example of Irish 'Gun Money' issued by James II in exile to pay his troops during the Irish campaign (identified by E. Besly). Tokens of this type, which appear to have been in fairly common circulation, include the month and year when minted: the token is stamped 'MAY 1690'. The intention was that they were to be exchanged, in the order they were issued, on the successful completion of the campaign and James's restoration. The 'XXX' on the reverse indicates 30 pence, or half-crown denomination.

Other finds

Analysis was restricted to material from deposits dating to Periods 1–3. A single item, an Iron Age glass bead, is of intrinsic interest and is described fully and illustrated. Metalwork, worked stone items and the fired clay are summarised briefly below with full details reserved for the archive.

Glass

A glass bead recovered from fill 1110 of pit 1008 (Pit Group 2) belongs to Guido's long-lived 'miscellaneous wave-decorated' class 5A (4th/3rd centuries BC to 6th/7th centuries AD). A Middle Iron Age date (*c.* 4th to 1st centuries BC) is suggested in this instance by associated ceramics. The earliest beads of this class are from the Arras burials of Yorkshire (Stead 1965, 59–60), which date to the 4th/3rd centuries BC. Geographically closer examples from Meare, Somerset, are perhaps as early as the 3rd century BC (Guido 1978, 63). This bead differs from these earlier examples in respect of its much greater size, which is however comparable with other Iron Age types. Untypical of the class as a whole is its strong cobalt-like colour and its opacity, although this may be due to decay (Eleanor Standley, pers. comm.)

Illustrated glass artefact (Fig. 5)

Approximately half of an annular glass bead. Opaque blue glass with white marvered white wave pattern. D-shaped section. Thickness 7 mm; diam. approx. 23 mm. Fill 1110 of pit 1008, Pit Group 2, Period 2.

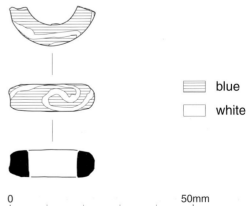

blue

white

Fig. 5: The glass bead (scale 1:1)

0   50mm

Metalwork

A total of 57 items of metalwork were recovered. The bulk of material relates to Period 4, with only fragmentary (and non-classifiable) iron nails or intrusive items from Period 3. Of note amongst the Period 4 material are 44 copper-alloy wire pins, mainly from deposits associated with the demolition and robbing of Building 1. Most examples are within the range 20–25mm, and as such are more typical of later 16th and 17th-century examples (Crummy 1988, 7). Remaining copper-alloy items include a lace end from robber trench 1062, which is typical of Crummy's non-riveted Type 2 and dateable to *c.* 1575–1700+ (ibid., 13) and a double-looped, rectangular-framed buckle from layer 1167, which probably dates to *c.* 1570–1700 (Whitehead 1996, 74). An iron knife retaining its plain bone handle, from robber trench 1062, is of post-medieval (probably 18th-century) bolstered form.

Fired clay and worked stone

Quantities of fired/burnt clay amounting to 3.5kg were recovered. All derived from Period 1 features and almost entirely from Pit Group 1. A single fragmentary clay loomweight of Iron Age triangular type was recovered from pit 1149, together with large, slab-like fragments of unknown function. The remainder (approximately 1.8kg) comprises generally formless fragments which probably represent burnt structural daub. A Norwegian ragstone whetstone of early medieval type was recovered from Period 3 cultivation layer 1124. Typically it has been perforated for suspension even though it is only 47mm long. It has clearly been worked down from a much larger whetstone.

THE BIOLOGICAL EVIDENCE

Animal bone, by Sylvia Warman

Animal bone recovered from Periods 1 and 3 was studied in detail. Measurements recorded follow von den Driesch (1976) unless otherwise specified. Material identified to species and element is presented and discussed in this report.

The hand-collected bone from Period 1 comprises 42 fragments, weighing 980g, and from Period 3 940 fragments, weighing 1.2kg (Tables 3 and 4). Totals for the number of identified specimens (NISP) and the minimum number of individuals required to produce the assemblage (MNI) have been calculated. In addition to the hand-collected bone, two Period 1 soil samples produced 307 bone fragments, weighing 31g, and three Period 3 samples produced 123 fragments, weighing 22g.

Table 3: Animal Bone, Period 1

Element	Cattle	Sheep	Sheep/Goat	Pig	Horse
Number of Identified Specimens (NISP)	12	1	16	1	6
Weight (g)	638	4	97	1	240
Minimum Number of Individuals (MNI)	1	1	3	1	1
% by NISP	33	3	44	3	17
% by weight	65	0.4	10	0.1	24.5

Period 1: Iron Age

The animal bone from Period 1 comprises cattle, sheep/goat, pig and horse (Table 3). The assemblage is small but consistent with the domestic fauna expected for this period. The cattle and sheep/goat remains show the widest range of body parts. The horse bones comprise limb bones and a couple of teeth; pig is represented by a single tooth. The soil samples produced sheep/goat, frog, vole and mouse. The Period 1 animal bone bears butchery evidence in the form of chop marks on nine bones from cattle, sheep/goat and horse.

Period 3: Medieval

The Period 3 assemblage includes cattle, horse, sheep/goat, pig and dog (Table 4), and is dominated by an incomplete dog skeleton from pit 1205 (Pit Group 3) and two largely complete horse skeletons from pits 1107 and 1229 (Pit Group 4). All bone was in good condition and well preserved. Such burials are not unusual for this period, and the

Table 4: Animal Bone, Period 3

MNI = Minimum Number of Individuals; NISP = Number of Identified Specimens

Element	Cattle	Sheep/Goat	Pig	Dog	Horse	Mole	Water vole	Chicken	Turdus
Head	8	11	5	3	70	1	-	-	-
Atlas	-	-	-	1	1	-	-	-	-
Axis	-	-	-	1	1	-	-	-	-
vertebra	-	-	-	34	73	-	-	-	-
rib	-	-	-	57	54	-	-	-	-
Costal cartilage	-	-	-	15	41	-	-	-	-
Scapula	-	-	1	2	4	-	-	-	-
Humerus	-	-	2	2	9	-	-	-	-
Radius	2	1	-	2	4	-	-	-	-
Ulna	1	-	-	2	2	-	-	-	-
Carpal	-	-	-	2	6	-	-	-	-
Metacarpal	1	1	4	6	6	-	-	-	-
Innominate	-	3	-	2	11	-	-	1	-
Sacrum	-	-	-	1	2	-	-	-	-
Sternum	-	-	-	-	2	-	-	-	-
Femur	-	-	-	2	9	-	1	-	-
Patella	-	-	-	2	4	-	-	-	-
Tibia	2	4	-	2	4	-	-	-	2
Fibula	-	-	-	3	-	-	-	-	-
Tarsal	2	-	-	12	16	-	-	-	-
Metatarsal	1	4	-	10	8	-	-	-	-
Metapodial	-	-	-	3	2	-	-	-	-
sessamoid	-	-	1	-	10	-	-	-	-
Phalanges	2	-	15	3	20	-	-	-	-
NISP totals	16	24	30	167	359	1	1	1	2
Total weight	720	195	253	796	10495.5	1	0.5	2	0.5
MNI	2	2	2	1	3	1	1	1	1
% by NISP	3	4	5	28	60	0.2	0.2	0.2	0.3
% by weight	6	1.7	2	6.8	89	0.008	0.004	0.02	0.004

examination of more or less complete skeletons provides the opportunity to investigate the size and type of animal used at the time. Table 4 shows the entire range of skeletal parts present from these animals, for which an accurate estimate of both age and stature has been calculated, and lists other species present in the Period 3 bone assemblage.

Pit 1107 contained the substantially complete skeleton of Horse 1, with bones from at least one other adult horse; pit 1229 contained the near-complete skeleton of Horse 2, and the foot of an immature pig. The withers (shoulder) height calculated for Horse 1 is 1.26m (or 12 hands 2 inches), the equivalent of a smaller modern pony such as the Dartmoor breed; for Horse 2 it is 1.30–1.37m (or 13 hands 1 inch), the equivalent of a medium-sized modern pony such as the New Forest breed. The latter is a very similar size to that deduced for horse remains found in a medieval pit at Stoke Road (Maltby 2002, 49). Horse 1 has some changes in the skeleton which appear to be the result of infection, including swelling and extra bone growth on the shaft of the cannon bone (metatarsal). Unusual bone growth can also be seen in the spine, where several thoracic and lumbar vertebrae are enlarged and fused together. This may have been the result of overloading, either from riding or use as a draft or pack animal. Dental wear on both horses indicates an age of least 12 years. The horse skeletons may well represent the burial of old or lame animals at the end of their working life. The dog from pit 1205 was an adult and is estimated to have had a withers height of 0.60–0.63m, similar to a medium to large modern breed such as a German Shepherd.

The medieval assemblage shows some similarities with the material from Stoke Road (Maltby 2002), although only domestic species were present there. The bone shows a low incidence of butchery marks as it largely comprises three partially articulated carcasses. Unlike the small quantity of horse bone from Period 1, which shows evidence of butchery and seems to relate to domestic waste, the horse bone from Period 3 has no butchery marks and represents the deliberate burial of entire or near-entire animals.

Charred plant remains, by Wendy J. Carruthers

Soil samples were taken from six pits (dating to Periods 1, 3 and 4) for the recovery of environmental remains, and processed using standard methods of flotation. The unsorted flots from six 10-litre subsamples were assessed, along with charred material sorted from the residues and small fractions of residues from samples <2> and <3>. Following assessment, Period 1 samples <2> and <3> were subject to full analysis of all 40 litres collected. Table 5 presents the results. The taxa recovered from the 10-litre subsamples from <1>, <4>, <5> and <6>, identified during the assessment, are also included as they provide information about the medieval and early post-medieval economies.

Although only small quantities of poorly preserved charred plant remains were recovered, a surprisingly wide range of possible crops is represented. The scarcity of chaff fragments and weed seeds means that there is little evidence for cereal processing and crop husbandry is present, and all of the charred material probably represents burnt domestic waste.

Period 1: Iron Age
Samples from the primary fills of Iron Age pits 1149 (Pit Group 1) and 1008 (Pit Group 2) were fully analysed. The samples were not particularly rich in charred plant remains. Pit 1149 contained evidence of oat (*Avena* sp.; although this could have been growing wild as an arable weed), hulled barley (*Hordeum vulgare*), emmer/spelt wheat (*Triticum dicoccum/ spelta*) and bread-type free-threshing wheat (*Triticum aestvum*-type). The same types of

Table 5: Charred plant remains, all periods

Habitat Preferences: A = arable; C = cultivated; D = disturbed/waste; E = heath; G = grassland; H = hedgerow; M = marsh/bog; R = rivers/ditches/ponds; S = scrub; W = woods; Y = waysides/hedgerows; a = acidic soils; c = calcareous soils; d = dry soils; n = nutrient-rich soils; o = open ground; w = wet/damp soils. All remains charred apart from (); cf. = uncertain ID; * = plant of economic value.

	Common name	Habitat	Sample no: 2 Context no: 1150 Period: 1 Feature: pit 1149	3 1110 1 pit 1008	1 1197 3 pit 1196	5 1056 3 pit 1055	6 1247 3 pit 1248	4 1167 4 pit 1167
Cereals (grain):								
Triticum aestivum/turgidum	bread/rivet-type free-threshing wheat	*	4	7	-	-	1	-
T. dicoccum/spelta	emmer/spelt wheat	*	1	6	-	-	-	-
Triticum sp.	indeterminate wheat	*	10	-	-	1	-	-
Hordeum vulgare L. emend.	hulled barley	*	3	11	-	-	-	-
Secale cereale L.	rye	*	-	cf.1	-	-	-	-
Secale cereale/Triticum sp.	rye/wheat	*	-	-	1	-	-	-
Avena sp.	wild/cultivated oat	*	1	-	-	-	-	cf.1
Avena/Bromus sp.	oat/chess	*	-	-	3	4	-	3
Indeterminate cereals		*	4	38	5	3	3	3
Chaff:								
T. dicoccum/spelta (glume base)	emmer/spelt wheat	*	-	1	-	1	-	-
T. dicoccum/spelta (spikelet fork)	emmer/spelt wheat	*	-	1	-	-	-	-
Cereal-sized culm base			1	-	-	-	-	-
Weeds:								
Corylus avellana L. (shell frag.)	hazelnut	HSW*	-	-	-	1	-	1
Vicia faba var. *minor* (frag.)	Celtic bean	*	-	-	cf. 3	-	-	-
Vicia/Lathyrus/Pisum sp. (4–5mm)	vetch/tare/pea	*	-	1	-	-	-	-
Legume pod frag.		*	-	cf.1	-	-	-	-
Odontites vernal/Euphrasia sp.	red bartsia/eyebright	CD	-	-	-	-	2	-
Sambucus nigra L. (seed)	elder	HSW*	-	-	-	(47)	(5)	-
Poaceae	small-seeded grass	CDG	1	-	-	-	-	-
		Total:	25	67	12	9 (47)	6 (5)	5
		Sample size (litres):	40	40	10	10	10	10
		Fragments per litre:	0.6	1.7	1.2	0.9 (4.7)	0.6 (0.5)	0.5

wheat and barley were present in pit 1008, along with possible rye (cf. *Secale cereale*) and possible pea (or a large-seeded vetch; *Vicia/Lathyrus/Pisum* sp.). Oats, rye and peas only start to appear in Britain in the Late Bronze Age/Iron Age period, so the appearance of all three in these small samples, albeit in low numbers and as poorly preserved tentative identifications, is not unexpected. In addition, bread-type wheat was surprisingly frequent in the samples, outnumbering emmer/spelt wheat grains (although numbers were low for all remains). Interpretation based on such poor assemblages must be highly tentative, but results suggest that Iron Age arable agriculture was advanced, at least in terms of the range of crops being grown. This may be because Bishop's Cleeve is situated on a small area of river terrace gravels surrounded by clay soils. This range of growing conditions will suit most crops: cereals like barley could be grown on the gravel, and wheat and oats on the clay.

Periods 3 and 4: Medieval and post-medieval

As with the Iron Age samples, the medieval and post-medieval samples produced small quantities of burnt domestic waste, most of which was poorly preserved. The evidence suggests that bread-type wheat, possible rye (*Secale cereale/Triticum* sp.), possible oat (*Avena/Bromus* sp.) and possible Celtic bean (*Vicia faba* var. *minor*) were being grown during the 12th to 14th centuries. The only cereal recovered from the Period 4 samples was possible oat (cf. *Avena* sp.).

There was no evidence to indicate that any of the sampled medieval features had been cesspits, which often contain mineralised plant remains (see Green 1979; Carruthers 2000). Several uncharred elder seeds recovered from samples <5> and <6> may have been partially mineralised (they were not modern contaminants as no embryos were present). If so, their preservation suggests that the diet was fairly simple, since no other fruit remains were present. The presence of charred possible Celtic beans and hazelnut shell (*Corylus avellana*) fragments is further evidence of a simple rural diet. Native hedgerow fruits and nuts would have added variety to the cereal and legume-based diet.

DISCUSSION

by Annette Hancocks and Martin Watts

The excavations have provided further evidence for the Iron Age, Roman, Anglo-Saxon and medieval occupation revealed over the past decade in and around the historic core of Bishop's Cleeve (Fig. 1). Although the excavation area was relatively small and the results of excavation relatively modest, the presence of Iron Age and medieval remains and the apparent lack of Roman and Anglo-Saxon features provide further evidence for the settlement history in the village. This is particularly so for the Iron Age features, which relate directly to features recorded at the immediately adjacent Gilder's Paddock excavation (Parry 1999).

Iron Age

It is now clear that the Middle Iron Age agricultural settlement identified at Gilder's Paddock extended southwards for a further 20m to 25m across the current site, and all the groups of features recorded here can be related to those found previously to the north. Pit Groups 1 and 2 here compare with Pit Group 1 at the south-west corner of Gilder's Paddock in terms of size and form (suggesting a primary function of food storage) and fill (suggesting a secondary function for the disposal of domestic waste). Although there was no evidence for a northward continuation of Gully 2, Ditch 3 here is clearly the southern continuation of Ditch 100 at Gilder's Paddock (Fig. 1; Parry 1999, fig. 2), and they possibly formed the north-west corner of a rectangular enclosure. Further to the south, Ditches 1 and 2 are on the same north-west/south-east alignment as the major boundary ditches 46/220 and 47/210 at Gilder's Paddock, and are clearly related.

The dating evidence recovered from the current site also supports the chronology suggested at Gilder's Paddock, where most features were dated to the Middle Iron Age, with some residual Early Iron Age material. The major north-west/south-east boundaries appeared to have been the latest features at Gilder's Paddock. Pottery suggested that the pit groups were probably out of use before they were constructed, and stratigraphically they were later than north/south Ditches 37 and 295 (Parry 1999, fig. 2, 99). At the current site, the pottery also suggests that the pit groups were the earliest features and the major boundary ditches were the latest, and they are more securely dated to the Late Iron Age than those at Gilder's Paddock, where only a single sherd of Late Iron Age pottery was recovered (ibid., 98–9). Although Late Iron Age material was also recovered from the other linear features (and associated pit) these were probably also earlier than the major boundary ditches: no relationship survived at the current site but the major boundaries at Gilder's Paddock clearly post-dated the smaller north/south ditches (ibid., fig. 2).

Interpretation of the Gilder's Paddock Iron Age remains as those of an agricultural settlement was based on the presence of food storage pits and boundary ditches for livestock management, and the recovery of quern fragments and animal bone (Parry 1999, 100). This interpretation is augmented by the evidence from the current site, where further storage pits and boundary ditches have been recorded, and where analysis of biological remains is also indicative of Iron Age agricultural settlement. While small, the animal bone assemblage is dominated by cattle and sheep/goat, the expected Iron Age domestic fauna, and the charred plant remains suggest that a wide range of crops were being grown including bread-type wheat, emmer/spelt wheat and hulled barley, and possibly oats, rye and peas.

Ditch 1 represents the southern extent of Iron Age activity at the current site, however, excavations on the southern side of Church Road (about 100m to the south of Ditch 1) have revealed further evidence for Middle to Late Iron Age settlement, including roundhouses, pits and postholes (Lovell et al. 2007). It is possible that both sites were parts of a single, substantial Iron Age settlement centred around Church Road, but it is more likely that they were separate farmsteads. They may have been part of a wider integrated network of rural Iron Age settlement, akin to that attested by cropmark and excavated evidence in the Carrant valley in south Worcestershire (Parry 1999, 100; Dinn and Evans 1990; Coleman et al. 2006).

Roman and Anglo-Saxon

No features of Roman or Anglo-Saxon date were identified but 12 sherds of Roman and 19 sherds of Anglo-Saxon pottery were recovered as residual finds from later features. The Roman pottery is consistent with assemblages recovered from other sites in Bishop's

Cleeve, including nearby Home Farm (Fig. 1), where evidence for sustained Romano-British occupation over several centuries was recorded, including ditches, pits, ovens and demolition material suggestive of a masonry building (Barber and Walker 1998). Roman remains immediately to the north at Gilder's Paddock, including a boundary ditch and linear inhumation cemetery, appeared to have been sited well away from the focus of occupation (Parry 1999, 101), and the lack of identified Roman features at the current site supports this interpretation. The assemblage of Anglo-Saxon pottery adds to the 17 sherds recovered as residual finds from Home Farm (Timby 1998, 134) and the 230 sherds recovered from south of Church Road (Lovell *et al.* 2007), which strongly suggests that there was a focus of Anglo-Saxon activity in the vicinity of that site.

Medieval and post-medieval

The medieval remains comprised a number of pits and a later cultivation layer. To the south, there was no evidence from the charred plant remains to suggest that the pits in Pit Group 3 were cesspits, though the large quantity of pottery sherds and animal bone recovered from them is indicative of domestic waste disposal, and one had been used for a dog burial. To the north, the pits in Pit Group 4 were dug for the burial of horse carcasses. The pottery from the pits, and from the cultivation payer that post-dated Pit Group 3, indicates that all of this activity could have occurred between the mid 12th to mid 13th centuries AD. The pits would be typical of the rear part of property plots fronting onto Church Road, although no trace of any medieval building was found. Similar groups of medieval pits were excavated at Stoke Road (Enright and Watts 2002), towards the rear (north) of plots adjoining the road to the south.

During the medieval period the manor of Bishop's Cleeve was under the lordship of the Bishop of Worcester, with a manor house at Cleeve Hall, parts of which date to the 13th century (Dyer 2002, 70). The 12th to 14th-century tofts excavated at Stoke Road were probably parts of peasant holdings on the western fringes of the manorial site (ibid., 71). The location of the Church Road site to the east of Cleeve Hall mirrors that of Stoke Road, and a similar interpretation seems reasonable, although the pair of medieval ditches recorded at Gilder's Paddock were thought perhaps to relate to occupation focused on the church of St Michael and All Angels, about 200m north-east of the current site (Parry 1999, 102). The animal bone and charred plant remains recovered from the current site are comparable to those recovered from Stoke Road, suggesting a similar level of subsistence.

Post-medieval activity was represented by the remains of Building 1 and associated structures in the southern half of the site. The function of Building 1 is unknown. It seems unlikely that this was a dwelling, which presumably fronted onto Church Road, but it may have been a food store to the rear, raised on dwarf stone walls and accessed by steps to the north-west. The date of its construction is unclear (it may have been later medieval in origin) but it was demolished and its foundation walls dug up sometime after 1690, and almost certainly during the 18th century. Development gathered pace during the 19th century with the construction of new buildings (probably a stable block or barn), cobbled yard surfaces, stone tanks and drains.